JOHN PATERSON

RECLAIMING the LIFE

We Lost Along the Way

 **FriesenPress**

Suite 300 - 990 Fort St
Victoria, BC, Canada, V8V 3K2
www.friesenpress.com

ISBN
978-1-4602-5541-4 (Hardcover)
978-1-4602-5542-1 (Paperback)
978-1-4602-5543-8 (eBook)

1. Body, Mind & Spirit, General

Distributed to the trade by The Ingram Book Company

TABLE OF CONTENTS

ACKNOWLEDGEMENTS

It is impossible to recognize everyone who has graced me with their patience, wisdom, encouragement, and support across the years culminating in the insights and life-lessons contained in this book. With deepest respect and appreciation, I thank you all for the parts you have played in my unfolding journey.

That said, I would specifically like to recognize the extraordinary contributions of my dear cousin Linda Davidson who has mentored and supported the often-times bewildering and difficult journey between my head and my heart, my dear friend Jason Spies who has left a permanent footprint on my back from challenging me to apply what I've learned, and my family of origin who have consistently and generously supplied me with space, encouragement, and every manner of support I required to dare greatly knowing they always have my back.

The beauty of embracing life is that it embraces you right back. May your unfolding journey of self-discovery and self-recovery open your eyes to the angels that walk beside you in the guise of family, friends, mentors, and—paradoxically—antagonists. Each serves the purpose of holding up a mirror so we can get a more accurate perspective of what we value. Through this expanding clarity, we make more effective choices that support our journey of improving the quality of our own lives and the lives of everyone we touch.

INTRODUCTION

Every commercial tells the same story a thousand different ways. The story promises, "buy this product or service and you will feel safer, happier, healthier." The implicit message is: if you want to feel better, you need something outside of yourself—something you don't already have and should therefore acquire. I, for reasons I will elaborate on, reject this story. My experience has demonstrated beyond a reasonable doubt that if we are to find genuine happiness and fulfillment in our lives, then the change that has to occur is internal, not external. Love, safety, purpose, meaning, self-worth, and self-respect arise from within us. Nothing outside of us can fundamentally alter our life experience until something on the inside changes first.

I wrote this book to describe how this shift from outside solutions to inside solutions takes place and the significant improvement in the quality of our life that occurs when this shift is achieved. To make this shift, we need to understand the process of possessing, losing, and finally reclaiming our true self. It is the discovery and subsequent recovery of our true self that enables us to experience the love, safety, purpose, fulfillment, and genuine happiness we've been seeking but have not found, until now.

The journey to create the quality of life we seek can be summarized as follows:

- We have a dual nature that is composed of two kinds of consciousness: one human, the other spiritual.

- Our human identity arises from our conditioned, ego-based consciousness, which creates our sense of self.

- Our spiritual identity arises from our unconditionally loving spiritual nature—our true self.

- Our highest purpose and greatest potential are realized by aligning these two identities into a single integrated identity whereby our ego consciously serves our spiritual nature.

- When this integration occurs, we develop the ability to encounter our own Unconditionally Loving nature. By reason of this nature, we seek to extend Unconditional Love—through our perceptions, emotions, and actions—into our own lives and the lives of everyone we touch. This is how Unconditional Love expresses and experiences Itself in living form.

- When we live from our spiritual nature to the best of our ability, the quality of our lives improves and there is an increase in our experiences of love, purpose, fulfillment, and genuine happiness.

- Encountering and extending Unconditional Love, in ways that are unique to each of us, is the path to realizing our highest potential and experiencing genuine happiness and fulfillment.

The underlying premise behind everything that follows is my fundamental belief that human beings need unconditional love to thrive, and we suffer terribly when we are cut off from it. In the interest of satisfying the essential need for unconditional love, human beings will go to extraordinary lengths. Our pursuit sometimes creates strange bedfellows and tragic consequences, yet the underlying motivation remains unchanged. We are driven by the overarching imperative to find and experience the unconditional love we need to be fulfilled and genuinely contented. Simultaneously, we seek to reduce our fear of being unloved or, more frighteningly, unlovable. This fear of being unlovable is tantamount to the death of our personhood. To live without experiencing and extending love leads to the living death of our own deepest nature. The whole range of human activity is directed towards securing a sense of safety, love, belonging, connection, genuine happiness, and fulfillment.

When referring to unconditional love, I include the widest possible range of its qualities and characteristics. It is the variety of forms unconditional love takes that offers us the greatest number of opportunities to extend and encounter it in our lives. Unconditional love is revealed through a myriad of qualities such as: trust, safety, dignity, respect, authenticity, meaning, purpose, genuine happiness, inspiration, gratitude, mercy, acceptance, humility, fulfillment, spirituality, creativity, consideration, curiosity, tenderness, forgiveness, open-mindedness, willingness, courtesy, inclusion, wisdom, compassion, empathy, friendship, and intentional silence, to name a few. In other words, unconditional love is expressed in a multitude of ways and is present whenever our deepest intention is loving kindness.

If our ultimate human imperative is to experience love, safety, purpose, fulfillment, and genuine happiness, and the means for achieving it is the successful integration of our ego-based and spirit-based identities, then our starting point is to assess and understand the nature of our present situation. See if any of these questions resonate.

- Have you ever questioned the story you've been told about how to be happy?

- Have you ever received a compliment and immediately thought of all the reasons it wasn't deserved?

- Have you ever been in a room full of people and felt completely alone?

- Have you worked hard to achieve a measure of success, as the world defines it, yet still feel that your efforts have failed to provide the love, safety, purpose, fulfillment, and/or genuine happiness you're seeking?

- Have you ever wondered: *Is this all there is?*

If you, like me, identify with some or all of these questions, then you may find value in exploring your mental models (Senge, 2006, p.180). Our mental models determine how we interpret the world, and these interpretations determine our experience. They have shaped your assumptions, influenced your judgements, and directed your behaviours until now. Mental models are the patterns of relationship our ego makes by drawing on our thoughts, perceptions, beliefs, values, feelings, and experiences. They help us organize and make sense of the vast quantity of information we gather from the people, circumstances, and situations we encounter throughout our lives.

For example, I had a mental model that wealth would bring me happiness. This pattern of relationships included: my thought that money would enable me to buy the things that make me happy, my perception that having nice things would bring me happiness, my belief that lacking money was the source of my unhappiness, my value regarding the relationship between money and personal safety, and my gut feeling that money provides power and power brings security. These all affected my personal experience of fear and insecurity when I was unemployed and unsure of how I was going to support myself.

Our mental models influence our behaviours, and our behaviours produce consequences. The sum of these consequences determines the direction our life takes and the experience we have of it. So long as we maintain a particular mental model, we act in alignment with it. When all you have is a hammer, everything looks like a nail. So long as I believed money would make me happy, getting money became my priority. But as the money came into my life, and I still experienced unhappiness, the only solution I had was to work harder to make even more money. Until I challenged the faulty assumption that money was the source of my happiness, I was caught in a self-reinforcing negative loop of continuing to do what I had always done in the failing hope that at some point I would secure the happiness I was seeking through increasing my wealth. This faulty mental model was the problem to be overcome. I was caught in an error trap wherein the harder I tried, the worse things became. It was only when I became willing to re-examine this model that a more effective approach to finding happiness became possible.

One of the goals of this book is to create opportunities for you to identify your mental models and the behaviours that flow from them. Which ones are serving you well and which are impairing your ability to improve the quality of your life? Identifying and replacing ineffective models with effective models is one of the keys to improving the quality of your life and increasing your level of genuine happiness.

Every human being carries the sum of every thought, experience, interaction, and consequence into their present moment. Whatever we are today is the result of every choice we have made in the past. These choices are the result of our existing mental models and the way we have interpreted our life and the world in which we live. Becoming curious about our models and interpretations opens the door to new ways of thinking, feeling, and acting thereby enabling us to identify more effective strategies for living in the future. Noted psychologist Gordon Allport describes this process as "purposeful striving which draws a person toward his chosen goals more effectively than any influences that push from the past." R. C. Leslie adds, "the future is not dependent on the past but is rather moulded by our conscious decision in the now." (Allport, G. as cited in Leslie, R. C., 1965, p.21)

Knowledge is not power. Only *applied* knowledge is power. It is the sum of the insights and decisions we actually put into practice that generates the consequences and experiences we encounter in our lives. If we don't like the results we are getting, we are perpetually free to make different choices. It is the quality of our choices that determines the quality of our life.

For those who have identified with particular concepts, ideas, or aspects contained in this book, I have included expanding self-awareness questions and an applied self-awareness exercise at the end of each chapter. These are offered as a resource to further explore and deepen one's understanding of the key concepts contained in each chapter.

The value you get out of this journey is in direct proportion to the changes you actually apply in your life. The sum of these changes determines the degree of improvement you achieve in your life-situation and the quality of life you experience in yourself and are able to extend towards others.

For the purpose of describing the developmental process for securing a better quality of life, I have segmented the book into four key themes: self-discovery, self-recovery, bringing our gifts to life, and the world beyond.

In *Self-Discovery*, we explore how the choices we've made up to now made perfect sense based on our interpretations and mental models at the time, yet they have not always been effective in creating the quality of life we desire. Reviewing and revising our interpretations and mental models results in changed behaviours, which change our consequences and experiences. The experiences we achieve become the standard for evaluating the effectiveness or ineffectiveness of our interpretations, assumptions, and mental models.

Self-Recovery shifts our perspective from exclusive reliance on our ego-based identity towards a powerful collaboration between our human and spiritual identities. Understanding and embracing this relationship is key to achieving the quality of life we desire.

In *Bringing Our Gifts to Life*, we learn that while all human beings share the same human and spiritual nature, each of us has a unique way of expressing Unconditional Love in the world. To the extent that we expand our connection with Unconditional Love and then consciously choose to extend it into our lives and the lives of everyone we touch, we not only achieve the purpose and meaning we seek, we also experience that special quality of loving fulfillment and genuine happiness that comes from realizing our unique potential.

Finally, *The World Beyond* describes the changes that occur as we begin living from our integrated self. Through this integration, our mental models, behaviours, and relationships with others and ourselves begin to change in the most remarkable ways. It is this shift from an ego-directed life to a spiritually integrated life that opens our heart and mind to the variety of forms through which Unconditional Love can enter our life and the lives of everyone we touch.

Through the conscious decision to be of service—to the best of our ability—to Unconditional Love, one day at a time we discover that the requirements to experience the meaning, purpose, genuine happiness, and deeply fulfilling quality of life we've been seeking was within us all along, waiting patiently for us to recover it.

With all my heart I invite you to take this journey with me so you can gain practical tools and effective strategies that allow you to let go of those things that interfere with your ability to recover the beauty and wonder of your own true nature. Through this recovery you will experience the richness and genuine fulfillment that a conscious life in voluntary service to Unconditional Love is capable of bringing you and—through you—to all those you encounter along the way.

Note to reader: I use the terms God, Unconditional Love, Higher Power, Power greater than ourselves, Him/Her/It, and Universe interchangeably. This is intentional, as I don't feel qualified to define the non-material Being which is not the universe but that thereby the universe exists. Please feel free to substitute whatever name/term reflects your beliefs.

Because of the confusion that frequently arises when discussing Religion, Spirituality, and Spiritual Being I offer the following definitions:

- Religion: The search for Divine connection through the acceptance of dogmas, rituals, and activities mandated and adjudicated by religious authority figures.

- Spirituality: The search for Divine connection through personal inquiry, experimentation, and application of Unconditional Love in all It's forms.

- Spiritual Being: One who consciously chooses to place her/his mind and body in the service of Unconditional Love.

PART ONE

SELF-DISCOVERY

CHAPTER ONE:

OUR HUMAN CONDITION

Human beings need loving relationships with others. Relationships based on acceptance, understanding, and authentic connection; relationships where we are free to be ourselves and to love one another—shortcomings, imperfections and all. No matter how hard we try to live self-sufficiently, the truth is we need each other. We encounter love in the company of others. This isn't a failing on our part; it is what makes us human. Desiring the loving company of others isn't an indication of some lack within, it is the evidence that human beings are social animals and we feel most alive when we are sharing our experiences with others. Our brains are literally hard-wired for social connection.

I can't count the number of times I've met people struggling to have more satisfying and meaningful relationships. People who feel they have to hide their true nature so others will accept them, and then suffer terribly because they keep this hidden-self locked away. We bury ourselves in disguises we think are necessary to be accepted. We tell ourselves that if people *really* knew us, or saw us the way we see ourselves, they would be horrified and reject us. So we move from interaction to interaction, never saying what we truly mean. We censor and sanitize it in an attempt to attract companionship. Even if that companionship is less than ideal, at least it's company.

The problem with this strategy is that these kinds of relationships are incapable of giving us the loving acceptance we need to feel truly connected. So long as we keep adapting to what we imagine the expectations of others are, we keep ourselves hidden away, and it is precisely these hidden parts of ourselves that we most desperately want to share with others so they can know who we truly are. The fear of rejection keeps us from taking that risk. And so we drift through life, never completely rejected and never fully accepted, and we grow more lonely and isolated.

To feel deeply connected with another human being, we need to share our whole story. But to share our whole story, we need to find someone we can trust—someone we feel safe around. That is our challenge. Whom can we trust? To whom can we tell our whole story who isn't going to judge and reject us? Who isn't going to tell us what to do, but instead will allow us to share who we are and, through their unconditionally loving acceptance, allow us to speak our whole truth out loud so we can hear ourselves say all the things we've kept buried inside us? The greatest of gifts that one person can give to another, the gift of listening with unconditional love and acceptance, is our deepest need and the solution to our loneliness.

Beyond this we also need to acquire the willingness and courage to examine our assumptions and mental models, to explore how we can break the grip of fear that dominates so many areas of our lives, and come to understand our true nature. I promise that you possess all the resources you need to acquire the life you have been seeking. They are within you right now, you just don't know what they are or how to effectively access them, but that is a temporary condition. As we progress on our journey of self-discovery and self-recovery, you will gain the understanding and life skills you need to begin creating and experiencing the genuine and deeply intimate relationships you've been searching for.

Authentic and life-enhancing interactions are possible. We can have the kind of relationships we desire, and the power to engage in those relationships is totally within our reach. We think we are dependent on the good opinions of others, but this is not accurate. It is a reasonable assumption given what we've been taught and have experienced, but just because it's reasonable doesn't make it accurate. It's reasonable for a person in tremendous emotional pain to turn to alcohol for relief, and for a short time it does dull the pain; therefore, it could be argued that getting drunk is a reasonable response to pain. Unfortunately anyone who's relied on this solution for a while discovers that the benefits are short-lived and that when the booze wears off they're right back in their hellish experience again. Getting drunk seems reasonable, but it's ultimately ineffective.

The way to test whether an assumption is accurate is to observe how it impacts our life, for better or for worse. For example, we might assume that the way to get accepted is to discover what others want from us and then modify ourselves to meet those expectations. While this strategy might provide temporary relief from our loneliness, the relief is short lived. We don't experience real friendship because by showing people only what we think they want to see, the person we really are remains hidden. This assumption prevents other people from encountering our authentic self, so even in their company we suffer the pain of isolation and loneliness. This is how we can find ourselves in a room full of people and feel completely alone, our experience of loneliness growing more powerful and painful. Our assumption may seem reasonable, but the proof that it's inaccurate is the fact that it doesn't actually deliver the results we want despite how reasonable and logical it seems to our mind.

We can improve the quality of our lives by observing and testing current assumptions and mental models to discover how they impact our lives. Which are accurate and effective, and which are inaccurate and ineffective, in bringing us the results we desire? As our understanding of these assumptions and models improves, we gain the power to adjust those that are ineffective. As we begin developing more accurate assumptions and effective models, our actions become more effective and the quality of our experience with others and ourselves improves.

The better we know ourselves, the easier it is to identify and secure our deepest yearnings. To get a more accurate understanding of the person we think of as 'me', we need to understand how the 'me' we think we are came about. Through understanding this identity, we gain the ability to make more effective choices to secure the quality of life we are seeking. In the next chapter we will begin this journey of discovery by examining how the ego constructs a conditioned identity and how this conditioned identity has shaped our view of the self we think of as 'me'.

EXPANDING SELF-AWARENESS

1. How willing am I to be compassionately curious about the parts of myself I am still hiding from others and myself?

2. What would change for me if I became willing to reclaim and share these hidden parts with others and myself?

3. What am I unwilling to share because I'm afraid of being judged unworthy of love?

4. Am I beginning to recognize that only through sharing all of me is it possible to get the genuine connection I desire?

5. How willing am I to trade my quantity of friends for fewer, more authentic friendships?

APPLYING SELF-AWARENESS

Take a sheet of paper and draw a line down the middle of the page. On the left hand top of the page write: "Parts of me that I am *willing* to show the world." On the right hand top of the page write: "Parts of me that I am *unwilling* to show the world." After listing as many parts of yourself that you are/are not willing to show the world, ask yourself the following questions:

1. How has keeping parts of myself hidden kept me safe?

2. How has keeping parts of myself hidden prevented me from having a deeper connection with others?

3. Which is more important to me: staying safe and cut off from genuine connection or taking the risk of letting people see all of me, knowing that some will reject me and others will love me exactly as I am?

4. How much value do I get from relationships that require me to hide parts of myself?

5. What emotions come up for me from this exercise?

6. Based on what I learned, what—if anything—will I change?

7. What do I hope these changes will do to improve the quality of my life?

CHAPTER TWO:

THE EGO-CONSTRUCTED IDENTITY

Our exploration of who we think we are begins with a powerful story. It is a story you learned and internalized, and it has influenced your thoughts, perceptions, feelings, and behaviours since the earliest stages of your life. It is the story of who you think you are; the story you created about yourself through the feedback you received from others. It is an ongoing, ever-changing amalgamation of thoughts, perceptions, feelings, and experiences that created and maintains your sense of self. It is the separate 'I' who exists independently of the world. The identity your ego continuously seeks to preserve is the constructed story of who you think you are.

What makes this story so powerful is that it has developed over the course of your life. While it is the only story you recognize as you, it is not, in fact, the whole story of who you truly are. It makes sense and is perfectly reasonable, given everything you've been told and have come to believe about yourself. There is no logical reason to doubt it, except that despite the overwhelming evidence you've accumulated, something doesn't feel quite right. It feels real, it makes rational sense, but it's incomplete. Something's missing.

You think you know who you are, but there's a nagging whisper deep inside you trying to get your attention. You're not quite sure what it is or what it means, but with each passing year you are becoming more certain that the life you're living is not the life you were born to live. If you were to guess, you might conclude that you're missing some vital piece of information that would significantly improve the quality of your life, if you could only figure out what the whisper is trying to tell you.

You are not imagining that whisper. Something deep inside you *is* trying to get your attention, and what it has to tell you is so important and so powerful it will open the door to a quality of life you can't presently imagine. It is your unconditionally loving spiritual identity trying to break through the story that you, and everyone else, have been telling about you. It understands that the only way for you to encounter and experience the life you were born to live is by breaking through this powerful story and reuniting yourself with the beauty, wonder, and power of your unconditionally loving nature.

So how is this transformation accomplished? It begins by understanding that the story of who we think we are is not based on a collection of objective facts but is our ego-based identity created by what we and others have told us about ourselves. Our first step is to understand how an ego-based identity develops in the first place. Let's consider the hypothetical case of Victoria.

When Victoria was an infant she couldn't distinguish between her inside and outside worlds. She was the whole universe. When people or objects came within the range of her senses, they became part of her universe. When they moved beyond the range of her senses, they ceased to exist for her. At this early stage in her life everything she wanted and needed simply appeared and disappeared. Victoria lived in the present. Victoria was authentic. When she was hungry, she cried; when she was tired, she slept; when she was awake, she wiggled around and grabbed anything within reach and stuffed it into her mouth (this being the primary method for gathering new information). What Victoria didn't realize yet was how dependent she was on others for her survival. She wasn't consciously aware of the world beyond her fingertips (or taste buds).

In time, Victoria began to realize that she was not the whole universe, that there were things quite independent of her influence. As this dawning realization began to sink in, Victoria became aware of fear. She began to realize that her comfort depended on gaining the cooperation of others. By paying attention to what worked and what didn't, Victoria gradually began to learn those behaviours that produced the results she desired and those that didn't. Being a resourceful baby, she stored all this information and became knowledgeable about the ways to behave to get what she wanted.

Unbeknownst to her, at the precise moment she began to realize that her wellbeing was dependent on others, Victoria's ego began constructing the opening chapter in the story of who it thought she needed to be in order to get her needs met. This was the moment she began separating from her authentic self and started to adapt her thinking and behaviours to gain the approval and cooperation of others. This was the birth of Victoria's ego-based identity. The Victoria who was a universe unto herself, who knew what she wanted and didn't hesitate to reach out to the universe to get it, gradually gave way to a constructed identity aware that her life depended on gaining the attention and cooperation of others to survive. Over time this ego-based identity became so automatic that Victoria started to see herself only in relation to this constructed identity.

As the realization of her dependence on others grew, her ego began noticing that certain behaviours were rewarded while other behaviours were punished. Victoria's ego didn't have a vocabulary to describe this cause and effect relationship. It intuitively recognized that certain behaviours elicited love, hugs, praise, and encouragement while other behaviours elicited anger, isolation, scolding, and fear. Victoria's ego also recognized that when she experienced love, her body felt warm and full and open on the inside. When she was denied love, her body felt anxious and rigid and defensive on the inside. Since her ego knew the experiences Victoria liked, and those she wanted to avoid, it learned to interpret her environment and adjust her behaviours to gain the love and avoid the disapproval of others.

Much of this transformation—from an integrated, authentic self to a constructed, ego-based identity—occurred unconsciously. It grew out of her ego's attempt to make sense of her world and to get her needs met, by whatever methods it could come up with, based on the information it received from the outside world. This is how Victoria's integrated and spontaneous relationship with the universe gave way to a fractured, constructed relationship.

Around the age of two, Victoria had two distinct identities. The self she came into the world with (her authentic identity) and the self she thought the world wanted her to be (her ego-based constructed identity). As her ego adapted to the wishes, needs, and expectations of others, she was no longer free to be authentic. The parts of her that were acceptable to the world remained visible and the parts of her that were unacceptable became hidden or lost inside her.

As she grew she acquired information from other sources. She discovered that her friends expected her to behave in certain ways or they wouldn't be her friends. In school she learned that her teachers expected her to behave the 'right way' to get the praise and recognition she desired.

Her religion taught her that certain behaviours were good and others bad, and if she wanted to go to heaven she'd better be good. On and on, from family to friends to school to church to her community, culture, and society. Victoria's ego learned that love, approval, and acceptance were conditional, and to secure them she needed to adapt to the requirements and expectations of others. The alternative was criticism, isolation, and occasionally outright rejection.

While the particular strategies our ego employs will be different based on external conditions of upbringing, nationality, gender, ethnicity, religion, political affiliation, socio-economic level, internal conditions of intelligence, emotional disposition, psychological make-up, etc., the goal is the same: to secure the love we need to grow and thrive. Regardless of the particulars, our ego discovers—at a very early age—that we are dependent on others for our survival, and finding a way to secure their cooperation and love is our ego's highest priority. In Victoria's case her ego determined that her happiness depended on gaining the approval of others, and the better she adapted to others' expectations, the more appreciated she would be and the more love she would receive.

For some people the ego-based strategies they employ to get the love they need are relatively easy and effective. These lucky few seem to possess a natural ability to seamlessly fit into almost any environment and thrive. For most of us the story is less happy. If we lack the particular talents, abilities, or social skills that are desired and celebrated by our family, community, or society, our struggle for love is much greater.

Convinced that our happiness depends on the good opinion of others, many of us find the task incredibly difficult. Lacking the looks, the brains, the creativity, the athleticism—whatever attributes or qualities are appreciated and rewarded by the people around us—we struggle to fit in. Our ego responds by working tirelessly to adapt and adjust our constructed identity to become someone others will accept and appreciate.

There are few limits to how far our ego is prepared to go to secure the love we need, and there is nothing wrong with this. We strive to encounter people who will reflect back to us that we have value and worth. That our life matters. That we are worthy of connection and love. To this end, every human being is ultimately driven. And so our ego does everything in its power to shape our identity and control our actions for the purpose of securing the love and connection we need.

The greater the difference between the qualities and characteristics we can access, and those admired and valued by the outside world, the more our ego attempts to adapt our identity to one that is more socially acceptable. The greater the adaptations, the further we move from our authentic self and the greater the level of stress we experience. The inadvertent consequence of our ego's best intentions is an increasingly stressful and unmanageable life-experience. Seen in this light, our ego is not some internal enemy to be overthrown and replaced. Our ego is simply leveraging every tool at its disposal to assist us in securing what we need to thrive.

Unfortunately Victoria didn't possess many of the qualities and characteristics that were admired and valued by her family and community. Victoria's ego did everything in its power to help Victoria fit in and get the love she was desperately seeking, but eventually she came to believe that she was a failure and unlovable.

She dropped out of school, then she left home. She fell through the cracks, and over time the story she told herself was that she was a worthless, unlovable, loser who was never going to amount to anything. She walked the streets. She started numbing the pain with booze and drugs. When her money ran out, she turned to prostitution. She joined a gang for protection. She participated in a robbery and someone died. She found herself sitting in prison, wondering how her life had turned out the way it did. Wondering why she did the things she did. She never wanted to live like this; all she wanted was to belong, to be loved. To be part of a community who accepted her as she was. Was that too much to ask?

Sound familiar?

Victoria is one story among billions. Look around and you will see that most people you know have adapted, to one degree or another, in an effort to belong. For many of us, the distance we've travelled from our authentic self to the constructed identity we have today is so great that we no longer understand who we are beyond this ego-based identity. The greater the adaptations, the greater the risk of judging our self a fraud. As this judgement sets in, we dread the possibility that people will discover our fraud and reject us, so we hide our fear—along with everything else—and our suffering multiplies.

We put on a mask and play a role, all the while hoping no one discovers our terrible secret. Often the stress of maintaining our role is so great that the only relief we get is through temporary distractions. Maybe its booze or drugs. Maybe it's gambling, over eating, sex, adrenaline, work, money, cynicism, or violence. We cope any way we can to deal with the internal pain of pretending to be what the world wants us to be while clinging desperately to the belief that this is the only way to get the love and connection we long for.

For some of us, the pain becomes so unbearable that we can't maintain the act any longer. This is the moment we realize we can no longer play this losing game. This is the moment when we are finally sick and tired of being sick and tired and become willing to change anything to relieve the pain that is our daily existence. This is the moment we hit bottom. Is Victoria's heartbreaking story required before we can change our lives? Absolutely not! Everyone has their own bottom, their own turning point. Each of us has a different capacity for pain, stress, adaptation, etc.

No one can tell you when you're ready to make a change. You are the only person who knows how you really feel on the inside. Despite the most glorious image you project on the outside—regardless of your success, fame, wealth, beauty, power, education—if on the inside you're holding the perception of a fake, a fraud, an unlovable human being, then all the external symbols suggesting otherwise are insufficient to improve the quality of your life. The whole world could scream from the rooftops that you are the most amazing person they've ever encountered, but if you believe the opposite on the inside, then they're all wrong and you're right.

If you doubt this claim, then consider the number of outwardly powerful, talented, and successful people who have self-destructed. How is it possible for their lives to appear so amazing on the outside, and yet they turn out to be so haunted, wounded, and broken on the inside that death is preferable to continuing doing what they've always done?

I'm not telling you anything you don't already know or at least suspect. The majority of us are trying to fit in to the best of our ability because we want to be accepted, valued, and most importantly, loved. The unexpected consequence of all this adapting is not only that we lose touch with our authentic self, but even when we succeed by the standards of the world, and get the respect and love we desire, we are not able to accept it. On some level we know that the person they're respecting and loving is an act we've projected into the world. As we become aware of this, we suffer even more painfully because we finally understand that the strategy our ego has employed to secure the love and connection we yearn for is the very strategy that prevents us from ever receiving it. The only way to genuinely receive the love and connection we want from others is to be who we truly are. It is to the precise degree that we are authentic with others that their respect and love can truly be experienced within us.

Our challenge is to recognize that long ago, so long ago we probably can't even remember, our ego created mental models that linked particular thoughts, perceptions, beliefs, values, emotions, and experiences to receiving love. It was these accumulated mental models that formed our ego-based identity. It is this constructed identity that we now recognize is incapable of securing us the love we desire. With this realization we find ourselves in a kind of no-man's-land between the authentic self we've suppressed and our ego-based identity that no longer serves us. With this realization comes a choice: continue doing what we've always done and hope for different results (otherwise known as insanity), or decide to review, and revise or replace our current mental models and operating assumptions with more effective ones that will move us towards becoming more authentic. This enables us to secure and experience the love and connection we seek and thereby begin living the lives we were born to live.

This process of identifying and testing our mental models and assumptions is how we grow and mature. Some of our greatest moments of growth occur when we test and revise models or assumptions that seem logical but that don't give us the results we want. Reflecting on the choices we've made and the experiences we've had, we come to understand that everything our ego's done has value because every experience provides us with useful information about what works and what doesn't work for us. This is how we leverage the riches in our past to improve the quality of our life in the present and future.

Based on everything we've been taught, our story—including the assumptions and mental models our ego has constructed—makes perfect sense. Each of us has made adjustments to get our basic human needs met. No one is an island. We need each other to survive and thrive. Improving our quality of life begins by recognizing that the way to truly get our needs met is to identify, test, and in some cases revise our assumptions and mental models. This culling process makes space for our authentic self to re-enter our daily life.

To the degree that we bring our authentic self into encounters with others, we begin to experience more intimate and rewarding relationships. Whatever love we receive can be *fully* received and experienced within. How ironic that securing the love we seek from others begins on the inside by letting go of our ego-identity's inaccurate and ineffective assumptions and mental models, thus restoring our authentic self within and to the world.

Based on this realization we can now turn our attention to discovering the identity our ego has constructed for us. With this understanding we can determine those aspects of our ego-identity that are either serving or undermining our goal of being more internally integrated and authentic—the prerequisites for increasing genuine happiness and fulfillment in our life.

DISCOVERING OUR EGO-BASED IDENTITY

One of the ways to discover our ego-based identity is to reflect on the ways we think and interact with the world around us. In our relationships with others, what behaviours and opinions do we share out loud and, more importantly, what behaviours and opinions do we keep hidden? In paying attention to the things we allow others to see and the things we keep hidden from the world, we gain a clearer and deeper understanding of what our ego believes to be true about us but unacceptable to the outside world.

Our ego makes these distinctions in an effort to make us more acceptable to others, thus increasing our chances for connection. Unfortunately as the gap between our visible and hidden selves expands, so too does our level of stress and discomfort. This widening gap leads to an increasingly unmanageable lifestyle. This juggling act is unsustainable because, as noted earlier, we begin to feel like our relationships are phony. This self-protecting deception prevents us from experiencing the love, trust, and intimacy we desire because only authentic relationships can generate these qualities.

The first step towards becoming more authentic in our relationships is to identify which aspects of our personhood our ego considers unacceptable. Once we've identified these aspects, we can begin exploring ways of reintegrating them into our visible life. The more aspects of our hidden self we can integrate into our constructed identity, the more authentic we become. As we become more authentic, the love we receive from others becomes more satisfying and fulfilling since it is offered to the person we truly are rather than the person we were pretending to be.

The integration of our visible and hidden self begins by compassionately exploring the mental models that guide our ego's decision-making process. The more we extend compassionate curiosity to our inquiry, the safer our ego feels, and the greater its willingness to let us explore its inner domains. The more we understand these domains, the greater our ability to identify and revise inaccurate mental models with more accurate and effective ones. Let's examine a specific case to illustrate how this kind of inquiry process might occur.

Beverly was visiting with friends who commented that she was getting very thin. In fact, they were growing concerned that she may be suffering from anorexia. In response to their concerns, Beverly did her best to put their worries to rest. "Oh, nothing to be concerned about. I wasn't feeling well the past couple of weeks so I wasn't eating much. I'm feeling much better now, so I'm sure I'll put on weight in no time." Secretly, though, Beverly was pleased. For her, being called anorexic felt great. From this encounter, Beverly received a valuable piece of information she could use to gain a better understanding of her ego-based identity.

Our ego uses feedback from others to shape our perceptions, beliefs, and behaviours. The feedback Beverly received from her friends informed her ego that her weight was a concern to them. From their perspective, Beverly's weight was potentially unhealthy; therefore, it was undesirable and needed to be corrected. To reduce the risk of being criticized, or worse, Beverly's ego adapted her response to lower their anxiety and calm their fears.

Often this kind of adapted response is the end of the experience. Our ego receives feedback, it interprets how that feedback is affecting our relationships, and it outwardly responds in the ways it believes will smooth over any tension generated by judgement. But what to do about that secret feeling of pleasure? How does Beverly's ego deal with this feeling of pleasure when the outside world is telling it her behaviour is a problem or even dangerous to her health? What is the truth in this situation, and what—if anything—should or might Beverly do about it?

One response is for her ego to suppress and deny her actual feelings in the interest of maintaining peace in her outside relationships. Regardless of what she may truly feel or think about her weight, her ego relies on its mental models and decides to project the response it thinks others want or need to hear from Beverly in order to maintain a peaceful, albeit inauthentic relationship with them. This is a struggle each of us endures as our ego juggles its mental models against the feedback it receives from the world and conflicting inner thoughts, beliefs, and feelings.

When inner conflicts occur, we are presented with another chance to discover whether particular mental models are accurate or not. Through these examinations, we identify ineffective models and gradually replace them with more accurate models. Over time we discover that our most effective mental models evolve through integrating our hidden self into our ego-based identity. The ultimate aim of our journey is complete alignment and integration of our spiritual (unconditionally loving) nature with our human (ego-based) conditioned identity. This enables us to improve the quality of our experience by increasing the degree of our authenticity and the amount of unconditional love we can encounter and extend.

So what is the process to better understand our ego-based identity and facilitate the transition from ineffective to effective mental models? Let's return to Beverly.

When we left her, Beverly was calming her friends' fears about her weight problem. On the inside, she was pleased by their judgement of her. Beverly's perception of her weight was radically different from her friends, but her ego concluded that if she revealed her true perception of the situation, the results would be negative. So, she decided to lie.

Without judging the good, bad, right, or wrong of Beverly's decision, to become more aware of her ego-based identity, she needs to thoroughly understand what she is telling herself about her anorexia without regard for how she or others might judge her. This is where compassionate observation becomes so important. If she is to discover the authentic truth about this aspect of her ego-based identity, Beverly needs to be able to investigate it back to its source. She needs the most complete picture possible of how and why her ego formed this mental model about anorexia and what she wants to do differently going forward, if anything.

The only way she's going to penetrate this model is if she can keep her ego feeling safe enough to let her get past its self-protecting defence mechanisms. Remember, whatever rationale supported the ego's construction of this mental model made perfect sense at the time. This is critical to understand. Our ego is doing the very best it can to interpret the world and develop strategies to bring us as much happiness and as little suffering as possible, so when we start investigating our ego's 'solutions' we need to recognize that it is working 24/7 to keep us safe and will bring the full might of its protective strategies into play the moment it feels threatened from the outside world or, more dangerously, from within.

For Beverly to discover the mental model that made anorexia a reasonable strategy to her ego, she needs to create complete safety for her ego so it will allow her to penetrate its logic to identify why it made perfect sense. She needs to discover how this model represented her ego's most effective, albeit ultimately ineffective, response to a perceived threat, need, or desire.

So how do we create the level of safety our ego requires for us to see into its deepest regions of model making? We start with a very clear commitment to our ego that we will accept everything we find along the way without judgement, prejudice, criticism, or condemnation. Our only objective is to see this model clearly, to bring a child's sense of wonder and curiosity. When our ego believes we are not a threat, and our deepest intention is only to understand—not change or ridicule—then the conditions are set for a journey of surprising and fascinating discovery.

One way to visualize this interaction is to imagine your ego as a deer you suddenly come upon in the woods. The moment you startle it, it runs away. The only way to coax it into the open is to help it feel safe. To explain past and present coping strategies, we need to understand the mental models that influenced those behaviours, and the only way to do that is to create enough safety so our ego doesn't feel threatened. One of the reasons our ego represses our thoughts is because it doesn't want us to experience the pain of self-criticism. The moment our ego perceives fear, danger, or criticism, like the deer, it bolts for cover.

The most important thing we need to remember is that everything we've ever thought, believed, or did made perfect sense at the time. It's easy to look backwards and judge our choices, but that's unfair. Our ego has always had our best interests in mind and has done everything in its power to provide the conditions that would multiply our happiness and reduce our suffering. The fact that it has not always been successful is not its fault. It has merely accumulated evidence from the outside world, done its best to interpret that evidence, and used all its power to bring us happiness. The Buddhists have a saying: "If we knew the whole truth behind every situation, our only response would be compassion."

I beg you to be compassionate and gentle with yourself. Our ego is not the enemy; it is simply struggling to figure out how to serve us best. The answers we seek are within us, and one step towards recovering them is to bring our ego loving kindness and compassion so we can get to the bottom of our mental models and the resulting behaviours. Once identified, we are then in a position to determine which models are no longer serving us and then to gently and compassionately release them, leaving space for more accurate and effective models. This is a life-long process. Our journey to encountering the authentic love and genuine happiness we seek is greatly advanced by bringing unconditional love to the investigation of our ego-based identity.

So what might this investigation sound like if we could eavesdrop on Beverly's internal inquiry?

"Wow, this is really interesting. These people are calling me anorexic, and while they think it's a problem, and some part of me agrees with them, what I'm aware of is, notwithstanding this 'problem', I am actually glad they're describing me this way. In fact, it makes me happy. I know that there's no way I can let them know this, but I'm really curious why their judgement makes me feel so happy.

What is it about being anorexic that I find so appealing? I wonder what I'm telling myself that would identify anorexia as a good thing when everyone I know defines it as a bad thing? Can I recall when I first became aware of my body weight? Can I remember how being thin was something I desired? Did it come from something I observed, something I heard, something someone said to me? Do I believe that being thin is somehow related to being good? To being beautiful? To being successful? Do I believe being thin is what I have to be in order to be attractive to others?

If I set aside every judgement related to being anorexic, for a moment, and just explore it without trying to justify or change it...what do I actually believe about it? What is it about being anorexic that I find appealing? Is this perception based on desire or fear? Is it about being more beautiful or needing to be in control over at least one area of my life?"

These are just some of the questions Beverly might ask to gain a better understanding of the mental model her ego has created regarding her anorexia. You can imagine how little progress she would make if her ego thought for a minute that she was going to beat herself up with criticisms and harsh accusations. Self-condemning judgements are one of the most compelling reasons our ego reacts defensively when we attempt to investigate our mental models. Remember, our ego's goal is to keep us safe, so you can imagine how resistant it will be to any hint of criticism. The only way we get honest answers from our ego is if we can bring a non-judgemental, compassionate, and genuinely curious attitude to our inquiry.

The questions I've imagined for Beverly are by no means exhaustive or even the questions you might ask yourself if you were in Beverly's situation. My goal is not to provide 'the questions' but rather to point you in the direction of the kinds of questions you might ask if you were genuinely curious about how your mental models were created.

Compassionate inquiry enables us to gain a deeper and clearer understanding of our mental models and how they came into being. Understanding them also helps us explain our behaviours that flow directly from them. Once we have as complete a picture as possible, we can then begin to explore whether these mental models still apply. Does this model, made so long ago, still serve me? If not, what—if anything—do I want to change? Put another way, if a particular model no longer applies or supports us, how might we gently and compassionately release and replace it with one that more accurately reflects and supports what we are learning as we journey towards integrating our lost or hidden elements with our constructed identity and with our spiritual nature?

This inquiry is an ongoing process of observation, reflection, and action followed by more observation, reflection, and action. The more aware we become of our mental models, the more we can identify which support and which undermine our goal of realizing our potential as spiritual beings having a human experience.

Compassionate inquiry is an effective approach for discovering our ego-based identity and supporting the ongoing alignment and integration of our human and spiritual domains. As we become more aligned and integrated, we begin to experience and extend greater love for ourselves and in our relationships with others.

EXPANDING SELF-AWARENESS

1. How willing am I to recognize that everything my ego does is intended to increase my happiness and reduce my suffering?

2. In what ways has my ego adapted my identity to get my needs met?

3. Which of these adaptations are limiting me more than they are helping me in achieving greater connection?

4. Knowing that being authentic is the key to experiencing love and genuine connection, how willing am I to become more authentic?

5. What one thing could I begin doing today that would move me in the direction of being more open and authentic with others?

APPLYING SELF-AWARENESS

On a sheet of paper write: "If I was willing to be more open I would…" then complete the sentence ten times, identifying what you would do that would help you be more open to new perspectives, opinions, mental models, and life-enhancing choices. On the backside of that sheet of paper write: "If I was willing to be more authentic I would…" then complete the sentence ten times, identifying what you would do to be more authentic in your interactions with others.

1. What emotions come up for me from this exercise?

2. Based on what I learned, what—if anything—will I change?

3. What do I hope these changes will do to improve the quality of my life?

CHAPTER THREE:

LETTING GO OF RIGHT AND WRONG, GOOD AND BAD

As noted in the previous chapter, our ego reveals its secrets only when it feels safe. One of the more effective ways for creating that safety is to set aside the terms good, bad, right, and wrong. These terms are unhelpful because they are loaded with cultural, social, religious, and moral implications that impede our ability to safely investigate our perceptions, feelings, and behaviours. The moment we judge our mental models and behaviours in terms of good, bad, right, or wrong, the underlying rationale gets buried beneath the weight of these judgements.

- "I better not go there, it's bad."

- "I know it's wrong to think that way."

- "It's for your own good."

- "What makes you so sure you're right?"

These judgements make it harder to uncover the thought processes that had our models making perfect sense to us at the time we created them.

If we are going to get to the source of our ego-based identity, we need to find ways to get past all the limiting judgements that frighten our ego, trigger its defenses, and leave us with nothing more revealing about our mental models than the recognition of their existence.

So how do we get past these terms? We can start by realizing that the terms themselves are not anchored in any permanent reality. If you reflect you'll discover these terms and their cultural, social, religious, and moral implications are subject to change over time. They are not absolutes that exist independently of the community in which we live, but are reflections of our community's current perceptions and attitudes. For example, it used to be considered a man's right to beat his wife and children, provided the weapon he used was no thicker than his thumb (thus the axiom *Rule of Thumb*). In most corners of the world, this behaviour is now considered wrong (thank God). Some people used to consider it wrong to teach black slaves how to read because it "spoiled" them. People in North America used to believe that it was good to promote the idea of the rugged individualist who "made it on his/her own." Others came to believe the concept was bad because it ignored the fact that no one achieves success without the help and support of countless others. A married woman was good, a divorced woman bad; homosexuals were bad and suffered from mental illness; the right and proper place for a woman was in the home. I used to believe that drinking was good for me because it relieved my mental and emotional torment. In time, I came to judge the same behaviour as bad because of the negative consequences that accompanied my drinking.

I could go on and on giving you examples from within families, religions, cultures, nations, etc., but I think we can safely conclude that the terms good, bad, right, and wrong are not absolute truths but relative interpretations. People develop different ideas over time about which perspectives, beliefs, feelings, and behaviours belong in each category.

If there are no objective definitions of good, bad, right, and wrong because the definitions change depending on who's defining them (and even within the same person they change over time), then for all practical purposes, the terms are useless as an accurate assessment of our thoughts, perceptions, feelings, and behaviours. If they're not accurate, and since they carry a lot of baggage that makes it difficult to evaluate the effectiveness of our mental models, then perhaps it makes sense to question whether we want to continue using them as guides.

Instead of judging our thoughts, perceptions, emotions, and behaviours by the changing standards of good or bad, right or wrong, what if we asked instead: "Is this mental model effective or ineffective when it comes to increasing my genuine happiness and reducing my suffering, and does it reflect and reinforce my true identity (a spiritual being having a human experience)?"

Evaluating our mental models by the changing standards of good, bad, right, and wrong merely informs us about our current interpretations and doesn't address the question of the actual benefits or harms created by them. In setting aside these futile terms and assessing instead whether our models and behaviours are effective or ineffective in helping us improve the quality of our life, we gain valuable information to assist us in deciding if a particular model is something we wish to maintain, revise, or replace.

EXPANDING SELF-AWARENESS

1. How have my judgements of good, bad, right, and wrong shifted over time?

2. In what ways do my judgements of right and wrong limit my ability to compassionately review and revise ineffective mental models and faulty assumptions?

3. What would change for me if I became willing to evaluate my mental models through the lens of effective or ineffective rather than right and wrong?

4. Am I beginning to see how evaluating my models and assumptions as effective or ineffective might accelerate my progress?

5. What model or assumption am I willing to examine through the lens of effective or ineffective without regarding my judgements of good, bad, right, and wrong?

APPLYING SELF-AWARENESS

On a sheet of paper, describe a time when you changed your mind about a situation you initially judged as bad but eventually came to judge as good. On the backside of that same sheet of paper, describe a situation you initially judged as right but eventually came to believe was wrong. Then, answer the following questions.

1. Based on what I learned about how my judgements have changed over time, how much confidence do I have in applying these standards of judgement to my perceptions, feelings, and behaviours?

2. Am I beginning to see how it makes sense to release my reliance on good, bad, right, and wrong and to evaluate my perceptions, feelings, and behaviours by the standard of whether they are effective or ineffective?

3. What emotions come up for me from this exercise?

4. Based on what I learned, what—if anything—will I change?

5. What do I hope these changes will do to improve the quality of my life?

CHAPTER FOUR:

HOW'S IT WORKING SO FAR?

Although change sometimes occurs because we recognize a potential opportunity for personal growth, more often we are dragged into change as a last resort when we finally conclude that our present way of living is incapable of meeting our needs. Until we have experienced sufficient fear, pain, or struggle, we tend to continue doing what we've always done. The trigger that awakens us from our business-as-usual approach to life could be a serious illness, the sudden death of a friend or loved one, or some other calamity. In my situation it was the pain of addiction—and my failure to manage it—that finally convinced me to consider a new approach to living.

Before we're willing to change, we need to be convinced that our strategies are incapable of bringing us the results we're seeking. When this realization triggers the moment of hitting bottom, we become ready to consider alternative ways of living. Willingness enables us to open our minds to the suggestions of people who previously hit bottom, and who are now experiencing the quality of life we desire.

Much to our surprise, the way forward is neither mysterious nor complicated. In fact, it's pretty straightforward, though not necessarily easy. It begins by having the willingness to accept that our present life is not working. Then, we start examining our current approach to living. With the help of others who have been where we are, we gain insights to identify the things we need to change. If you are unsatisfied with your life, then you are ready to proceed. If you haven't reached this point yet, then I urge you to continue doing what you've always done until you become convinced that your best ideas are incapable of bringing you the quality of life you want.

There is a term that explains the source of the struggle we experience before we become willing to change our thinking—error trap. An error trap occurs when an underlying assumption is inaccurate or a mental model is ineffective. When we act on a faulty assumption, every decision that follows takes us farther away from the results we're seeking. The way to determine if an assumption or model is an error trap is to observe what happens when acted upon. If it is an error trap, then the situation will get worse. For example, when I was a teenager I felt like I didn't fit in. I was shy, awkward, and insecure. At high school dances I hovered by the entrance. Afraid of being rejected, I never dared to ask a girl to dance. Trapped in my shell of fear, all I could do was look on and secretly hate the boys who danced with the girl I wanted to be with. It was around this time that I discovered booze. The first time I got drunk I decided that I had discovered the answers to all my prayers. When I was drunk I felt amazing. I was invincible. I could do anything! My shyness and insecurity disappeared. It took me eight years to discover that this "solution to all my problems" was in reality a huge error trap. Operating under the faulty assumption that booze made up for my inadequacies, I did everything in my power to get it and drink it. The fact that I occasionally had to steal it or steal money to get it wasn't important; I believed I couldn't be who I wanted to be without it. My wellbeing depended on it, and the only time I felt at peace was when I drank. Over time my life turned inside out. As I spent more and more of my time drunk, my sober life grew worse. I was literally replacing my sober life with the fantasy life I had while drinking.

I remember the occasion when my error trap was revealed to me in the starkest way. I was drinking on the floor of my apartment and listening to a rock album by my favourite keyboard artist, Rick Wakeman. He was performing *Journey to the Centre of the Earth* with the London Philharmonic Orchestra. As the finale approached, the music soared, the cymbals crashed, and the orchestra played to a thunderous climax. As the last note struck, the audience erupted into applause. Through the power of my imagination and the magic of intoxication, it was me—not Rick Wakeman—that people were applauding, and I was amazing!

The rude awakening happened when the record ended and I opened my eyes. In front of me was my bottle of sherry spilling onto the carpet. My ashtray was overflowing with cigarette butts, and as I drew my eyes to the other side of the room I saw my piano sitting against the wall with the lid closed. At that moment, I had the completely sober realization that not only was I *not* Rick Wakeman, I hadn't played my piano for the past six months. I was living a lie. I was living in a drunken fantasy, and my sober life was becoming a wasteland.

The force of this realization filled me with fear and self-loathing. I was a fraud, a fake, a drunken loser. I would be better off dead. This was the error trap playing itself out. My solution was taking me to hell. The more I relied on it, the worse my life got, and that only further motivated me to get drunk. In this moment I realized I couldn't deceive myself any longer. I knew, in the core of my being, I couldn't carry on. I didn't know how to live in the sober world, and my drunken fantasy world had just blown up in my face. I couldn't stand my sober life, and I couldn't keep drinking. Death seemed like the only way out, but I was afraid of the pain. Thinking I was probably insane, but having nowhere else to turn, I desperately reached for help. That moment, I hit bottom. But in that same moment, my life began to improve, though it would take many months before I realized it.

Not all error traps are this dramatic but each shares the common feature of taking us farther away from the outcome we desire.

THE ERROR TRAP OF APPROVAL SEEKING

Error traps can be very subtle and powerful. This is particularly the case when we are exposed to them at an early age and by people we believe know better than us. One of the most powerful error traps that begins when we are growing up is the belief that the approval of others will increase our happiness and self-worth. This error trap entices our deep need for belonging and acceptance in the world. The problem is that it not only requires us to adjust our behaviours to "gain" the approval of others, it implies that our sense of wellbeing and happiness depends on how others perceive us. Let me share a personal example that demonstrates, in the clearest possible terms, the potency and suffering that comes from the error trap of approval seeking.

A situation arose where someone gossiped about me. I discovered this when another person informed me that they no longer wanted to be my friend because of the things they had heard. Initially I was very hurt and angry. I had never experienced the pain of gossip before, and I couldn't believe I was on the receiving end of it now. I was furious. I wanted an explanation. I wanted a retraction. I had been harmed, and I wanted justice. Naturally all these thoughts and emotions came flooding through me like a tidal wave. But instead of impulsively reacting, I knew that the most effective course of action was to do nothing. I recognized the force of my emotions, and knew that I couldn't trust them to provide me with an effective solution. Any decision made in the heat of anger was bound to be destructive and would merely aggravate an already difficult situation.

While this period of doing nothing was really difficult, I trusted that my Higher Power would provide me with a solution. In the following days, I asked my Higher Power for understanding. I have come to recognize that everything that occurs in life has a pearl of wisdom embedded within it, if we only have the patience to discover it. Despite the anger and pain, I absolutely believed this situation was no exception. I framed my request to my Higher Power this way:

"What are you trying to teach me here? What is the wisdom buried within this experience? What am I supposed to learn, and how do I put it to use in such a way as to convert my anger and pain into something beneficial?"

As I sat reflecting on these questions, still writhing in my anger and pain, a conversation popped into my head.

You're really angry and hurt by this gossip, aren't you?

"Damn right I am!"

Well, why are you so angry?

"I've worked my whole life earning the trust and respect of others, and in one moment someone has attempted to undermine my reputation."

So what you're saying is that you've worked your whole life to gain the approval of others and now that that approval has been threatened, you're hurt and angry?

"Yes, that's exactly what I'm saying. What right does anybody have to gossip about me? How dare someone try to destroy my reputation."

Okay, I understand your point. So, let me ask you another question. If you've been working your whole life to get the approval of others, by developing your reputation, does that mean that your sense of self-worth is determined by how others perceive you?

"I suppose it does. Otherwise it wouldn't matter what other people thought or said about me. And based on the amount of anger and pain I'm feeling, I would have to conclude that yes, my self-worth is strongly impacted by the opinions of others. The better their opinion of me, the better I feel about myself."

Well, what about your opinion of yourself regardless of what others think or say about you? How do you feel about yourself? Do you experience yourself as a worthwhile person?

Do you know that you have honour and dignity whether anyone else thinks so or not? If you were the only person alive on the planet, how would you feel about yourself? In other words: who are you, independent of the opinions and judgements of everyone else on the planet?

Who is John in the deepest core of his being? Is John a person of worth and dignity even when the world says otherwise? In fact, does their opinion of you actually change the truth of who you are in any way? If not, then is it possible that the pain and anger you're feeling about this gossip is actually the result of your over-reliance on the opinion of others, since who you are isn't altered by anything the outside world suggests to the contrary? Is it possible that the anger and pain you're experiencing is only possible to the extent that you are seeking the approval of others to provide you with your own sense of wellbeing?

If you were confident about who John truly is, and you were content and secure in the knowledge of your self-worth, then isn't it reasonable that the gossip of others wouldn't hurt you in the least because you would be at peace with the knowledge of your true self regardless of their opinions of you?

"Yes everything you're suggesting is logical and reasonable. I can see from your line of inquiry that the pain and anger I'm experiencing isn't really about the gossip, it's about my reliance on the opinions of others to supply my sense of self-worth. I had no idea how important their opinions were to me, but the intensity of my emotional reaction clearly shows just how dependent on the opinions of others I've been to validate that I'm a person worthy of trust and respect."

As a result of this internal conversation, my journey forward became obvious. My first step was to begin learning how to experience loving thoughts about myself from within myself. Then I had to stop relying on the opinions of others to validate my self-worth, because as this experience clearly demonstrated, I have absolutely no control over how the world chooses to judge me, and trying to control their opinions is impossible.

Through this period of reflection and dawning realization, I gained tremendous insight into the error trap I hadn't even realized I was caught in. It was an extraordinarily painful learning experience, but I now realize that the only way I could have discovered the degree of my reliance on the good opinion of others was to have that opinion undermined. As the result of experiencing the degree of anger and pain I felt, I had indisputable evidence of my core problem. It wasn't being gossiped about that was the real problem, it was my over reliance on the judgement of others to secure my sense of self-worth. This was my error trap. The gossip and my intense emotional reaction were the mechanism and evidence that revealed it.

Ironically, and in keeping with the nature of how Unconditional Love seeks only to multiply itself, I came to regard the gossiper as one of my greatest spiritual teachers. If it hadn't been for the gossip, I would never have discovered just how dependent I was on the good opinion of others to provide me with my sense of self-worth.

Discovering the error trap of approval seeking, I started wondering how I could learn to validate myself independent of the opinions of others. I started by reflecting on the fact that God's opinion of me has never changed. God is not influenced by gossip. The idea is ridiculous. So if God's opinion of me has never changed, then to the extent I could begin seeing myself the way God sees me, I could become increasingly independent from the opinions of others. The source of my self-worth would emerge from within.

My challenge, and growth opportunity, became one of learning how to see myself as God sees me. I found myself praying, "God, help me to see myself through your eyes." By paying greater attention to the thoughts I was holding about myself, in time I gradually became less and less reliant on the opinions of others, and a growing freedom and inner joy began to replace the fear of: "What will people think of me?"

As my encounter with my own loving nature expanded, the freedom to be myself when dealing with the world also expanded. No longer striving to secure the approval of others, I began to explore what John really thinks, feels, and believes without regard for the judgement of others. It was as though I suddenly woke up from a dream in which I had been held hostage to outside opinions of me. Fully awake, I discovered and affirmed that I—along with everyone else—am a spiritual being, arising out of Unconditional Love. I gained the freedom to act more authentically as my experience of self-worth shifted from the outside world to the inside. Not only did I gain the benefit of feeling better about myself, I also discovered the ability to encounter and extend my unique expression of unconditional love in the world.

There is no way I could have come to this realization and condition of peace and loving contentment unless the error trap I had been operating in was exposed. The damage to my reputation, caused by gossip, was the critical trigger that revealed just how invested I was in this error trap. So, when I state that I came to think of the gossiper as one of my greatest spiritual teachers, I'm not exaggerating or trying to put a noble face on this painful experience. It is a simple fact. While I would never have volunteered to go through the pain and emotional suffering I experienced, I know now that it was absolutely necessary to awaken me from the powerful error trap of approval seeking. My quality of my life has improved immeasurably as a result of this discovery.

Imagine the most loving experience you've ever had, and then imagine it expanding in scope and intensity to infinity, and then you will have an idea of the degree of love that God feels for each and every one of us. Regardless of how others have judged you, and more damagingly how you are judging yourself, you have been and always will be unconditionally loved by God. God doesn't make junk. Your very existence is proof of your lovability because you couldn't exist if Unconditional Love didn't will it.

THE ERROR TRAP OF CONTROL

Another powerful error trap we need to confront on our journey to genuine happiness is our belief that the more control we have over our life and the world around us, the greater are our chances of being secure and happy. This has been drummed into us since we were old enough to understand the concept. Control equals power, freedom, and independence. What child doesn't yearn to become an adult so they can call their own shots? What child doesn't believe that the greatest thing about being a grown-up is that they get to do whatever they want?

From a child's perspective, this is a fact. Most adults smile at the idea. "Yeah, right. Just wait. You'll discover that being an adult is a lot different than it looks from where you're standing." Only with the perspective of adulthood do we recognize how naïve and flawed our childish perception of adult freedom was. Only later do we understand the number of forces that shape and govern the choices that adults regularly confront. But there is no way for a child, holding a child's point of view, to understand and truly appreciate what is involved in adult decision-making.

In the same way, our perception of control makes perfect sense holding our current mental models, but just because they seem perfectly reasonable doesn't make them accurate. If our journey from childhood to adulthood has taught us anything, it is that things appearing certain can suddenly change as new information becomes available. In the same way, when we begin to bring a more inquiring mind to the subject of control, the certainty that we felt begins to waiver. Unexpectedly what seemed reasonable begins to feel far less reliable. As our experiences accumulate, the idea that we have the ability to control our lives, or the lives of others, becomes less and less believable.

I remember one such occasion when I was brought face-to face with this particular error trap. I received a message from my boss that the CEO had been called into the bank to be informed that if the company didn't come up with eight million dollars in the next 30 days, the bank was going to shut down the company and everyone would be out of work. This news freaked me out. Immediately my mind went into overdrive. As the sole provider of a young family of four—a mortgage, a car loan, credit card debt—I was concerned. What was I going to do if I lost my job? How would I provide for my family? How would I pay my mortgage? What if the bank foreclosed on us? Where would we go? What would we do? How much money did I have in the bank? What about my pension contributions? Could I get access to them? What if I couldn't? How would I tell my wife? What would I tell the kids? How would I be able to protect them? How was I going to get a new job in time to avert financial disaster?

On and on, questions raged through my mind. For every solution, ten new problems. Within a few hours I realized there was simply no way for me to control all the things that might occur if I lost my job. There were too many unknowns and too few answers. I was being sucked into a situation not of my own making, one I had never anticipated or even considered.

I was a really good employee, and the idea that I might lose my job had never crossed my mind. But here I was, facing what felt like disaster, and I couldn't do anything about it. This situation was entirely out of my hands; I had no ability to control it. Confused, I couldn't think of a single thing to do, so I just sat there, staring off into space with no answers or ideas of how to relieve myself of this overwhelming sense of powerlessness.

Fear quickly turned to helplessness, and then depression set in. My brain was exhausted. I stared off into space for about thirty minutes. Nothing came into my mind. At some point I did the only thing I could think of. "God help me." As I continued sitting there, a thought popped into my head. "Let's look at this the other way around. What exactly do you have control over?"

As I started thinking about the things I did have control over, I discovered that it was pitifully few. No control over my job security, over how my family would react, over what the bank might do… In fact, if I was completely honest, I didn't even have control over whether I would be alive in the evening. I assumed I would get in my car and drive home safely, but I couldn't know that for a fact. Every day people going from one place to another never reach their destinations. For all I knew, I could get into an accident on the way home and not survive my injuries. My continued existence was an assumption, not a fact.

As this reality began to sink in, an amazing thing occurred. All my anxiety, fear, and paralysis started to bleed away. I could see, in the clearest possible terms, that the source of my fear wasn't really the job situation or how my family might react or what the bank might do. I realized I had been operating within the error trap that I was in control of my life. When news of the impending bankruptcy suddenly exposed my vulnerability and revealed the actual degree of control I had over my job security—and most other things, for that matter—the illusion burst like a balloon. I was deluding myself. I wasn't in control of my life. Sure, I could make decisions, but the outcomes were totally out of my control. I lived my life based on a set of assumptions that could change in a heartbeat, as this situation proved all too clearly.

As this deeper truth began to penetrate my mind, I asked myself: "Realizing what you now know, is there anything you do have control over?" As I mulled this over, I remembered a book I read called *Man's Search for Meaning* by Viktor Frankl, who survived two and a half years in four Nazi concentration camps. One of the things he realized on his first night in the camp was that "when everything is taken from you…the only thing you have left is the power to choose your response to the situation." From the moment this thought penetrated my consciousness, I knew this was the key.

It is true that I had very little control over the things that may or may not occur in my world. But my response was something absolutely within my control. I began thinking, "What is the most effective response I can have in this situation?" It was obvious that there was nothing I could do about the company, so I decided to focus on supporting my staff, all of whom were also scared out of their minds by the news. I could focus on doing everything in my power to help them deal with their fears by shifting their attention from things they had no control over to the one thing they could control…their responses.

This shift in thinking brought a tremendous feeling of optimism. Suddenly it was clear to me that I had been paralyzed by my fear of losing control when the reality was that most of the control I imagined I had was an illusion. Knowing that how I chose to respond was the one real power I had, I chose to trust my Higher Power to see me through this unpredictable situation, and focused my energies on supporting my staff.

As is frequently the case, the company restructured, paid the bank, and everyone kept their jobs. As an unexpected benefit of this crisis, when the consulting company came in to restructure the organization, I decided that the most effective response was to completely embrace the change process and learn everything I could about how companies restructure. It was the most amazing learning experience in the world of business I had ever participated in, and I got to experience it from the inside out. I learned more about business than I had ever known, and the quality of that education continues to serve me to this day. I am forever grateful for the education I received as the result of choosing to embrace that process of change. The one power I had proved to be the only power I needed.

Through the process of fear and paralysis, reaching out to the God of my understanding, and recognizing and revising my mental model of control, I was able to convert this crisis into one of the most powerful and beneficial experiences I've ever had. I never would have volunteered for this lesson, but I am thankful for the insights that came out of it and the many unexpected benefits that continue to reverberate in my life today.

This is precisely how a crisis can be converted into a benefit. Letting go of our illusion of control and reaching out to our Higher Power sets in motion a chain of thoughts, decisions, and behaviours that are filled with opportunity and benefit. But first we must be willing to set aside our faulty assumptions, our imaginary fears, and our delusions of control, and ask God to guide our responses. If we accept the responsibility of choosing our responses, and trust that there is a pearl of great value hidden within every situation, then the results of the inevitable crises we encounter in our lives can become a source of tremendous learning and long-term benefit. For this to occur we need only to align our thoughts and actions with the guiding influence of a power greater than ourselves. Trust that everything that happens in our lives contains seeds of unrealized potential and opportunity.

If you are wondering if any of the assumptions or mental models that direct your thinking and behaviour are error traps, then simply start paying attention to the consequences they produce. If you are caught in an error trap, it will ultimately reveal itself by creating an increasingly unmanageable experience for you. With every assumption or mental model you're holding onto, the question to ask yourself is: "How's it working for me so far?"

To further pinpoint potential error traps and faulty mental models, it is useful to take stock of our dealings with ourselves and others, identifying which aspects of our living strategies we want to hold on to and which we want to let go of. We will explore this more deeply in the next chapter.

EXPANDING SELF-AWARENESS

1. How does seeking the approval of others limit my ability to be authentic?

2. Being completely honest, what do I think and feel about myself and my relationship with the outside world?

3. What matters most to me?

4. If there is a God, do I believe Her/His/Its opinion of me ever changes?

5. Do I accept that I cannot change anyone without their cooperation?

APPLYING SELF-AWARENESS

Take a sheet of paper and draw a line down the middle of the page. On the left hand top of the page write: "Things I have control over." On the right hand top of the page write: "Things I don't have control over." After listing as many control/no control elements as you can think of, answer the following questions.

1. What people and situations am I trying to control that I don't actually have control over?

2. How does trying to control things I have no control over affect my life and the lives of those I am trying to control?

3. How would letting go of control and focusing on choosing an effective response change the way I relate to others?

4. What emotions come up for me from this exercise?

5. Based on what I learned, what—if anything—will I change?

6. What do I hope these changes will do to improve the quality of my life?

CHAPTER FIVE:

TAKING STOCK

If you're caught in one error trap, chances are you're caught in others. It is the behaviours that flow from our error traps that create much of the struggle we experience. It is an error trap that convinces us we've got to stay in control, even as life becomes increasingly unmanageable as the result of acting on it.

The purpose of an inventory is to thoroughly identify as many error traps as possible, so that they can be revised or replaced by more accurate mental models that actually improve the quality of life rather than creating greater chaos and distress. We can't revise error traps we don't know we're acting on.

Taking a personal inventory, which you will do at the end of this chapter, is one way to make sense of the choices you've been making up to now. Through the exercise you will identify the assumptions and mental models you've been depending on to get the results you want. While every one of them made perfect sense at the time, the inventory will help you identify which are assisting you and which are undermining your ability to achieve the results you desire.

It is critically important when conducting your inventory that you exercise great self-compassion regarding everything you've done up to now. While your actions may appear to have been illogical or indefensible, the reality is that this judgement is only possible from the vantage point of hindsight. You couldn't have known at the time that a particular assumption or mental model would produce negative results. Nobody sets out to delib-erately screw up their life, so be gentle with yourself. The inventory isn't a tool to beat yourself up with. Rather, it gives you a more accurate view of the assumptions and mental models you've been holding, the choices you've made, and the results you have achieved through them. Based on what you learn, you can decide which you want to continue using and what—if anything—you will do differently with those that are undermining your ability to get the results you want.

It is only through compassionate inquiry that we can fearlessly scrutinize our assumptions and mental models to discover how they influence our behaviours and the outcomes we experience. Accurate self-knowledge precedes effective change. As Kierkegaard noted, "Life can only be understood backwards; but it must be lived forwards."

Our assumptions and mental models influence us in ways that are sometimes obvious, such as through the people we choose to hang out with. Sometimes it's very subtle. For example, "Why do I continue to seek the approval of people I don't even like?"

Having examined our assumptions and mental models, our next task is to expand the scope of our inquiry to consider the judgements we hold about particular people, places, and events. Why do we hold the judgements we do? This is the subject of our next inquiry, and it may surprise you to discover what our judgements are really telling us.

EXPANDING SELF-AWARENESS

1. Am I willing to let go of my error traps and to replace them with more accurate assumptions and mental models?

2. How can I expand the influence of those assumptions and mental models that are supporting my quality of life?

APPLYING SELF-AWARENESS

Take a sheet of paper and create three sections by drawing lines vertically down the sheet. Label the sections **Activity**, **Impact**, and **My Part**, respectively. Under **Activity**, list activities that are causing you distress. For each, describe in the next column (**Impact**) how it is impacting your life. Under the third column (**My Part**), identify the assumptions or mental models (error traps) that justify and/or maintain each activity. Identify as many assumptions and error traps as possible. Next, shift gears and repeat the exercise on the backside of the paper, this time listing activities and identifying the assumptions/mental models that bring you joy, satisfaction, fulfillment, etc. Once you've completed your inventory, answer the following questions.

1. What did I learn about myself based on my inventory?

2. Which assumptions and mental models are producing positive results for me, and which are not?

3. What emotions come up for me from this exercise?

4. Based on what I learned, what—if anything—will I change?

5. In what ways do I hope these changes will improve the quality of my life?

CHAPTER SIX:

WHO'S JUDGING WHOM?

Believing that the judgements we hold about others have anything to do with them is an error trap. The error is believing that our judgement of others relates to them. It doesn't. It merely serves as the catalyst for helping us uncover our own assumptions, preferences, and mental models. The judgements we hold about people, places, and things are a reflection of our worldview and have virtually nothing to do with the targets of our judgements. If you doubt this claim then simply observe a group of people interacting and notice how different people have different reactions (judgements) to the same situation. You will quickly discover there are as many different judgements about the situation as there are people. The reason for the variety of judgements is that each individual is projecting their own assumptions, preferences, and mental models onto the situation while thinking they are stating an observable fact. Nothing could be further from the truth.

We judge people, events, and things continuously. We have to. If we didn't, we wouldn't be able to make decisions. It is our ability to identify preferences, make relative distinctions, and apply different emotional weight to various choices that enables us to make a decision. What outfit will I wear to the funeral? Where will I go on my vacation? Do I want to go alone or with someone? Do I want to take this relationship to the next level?

Making judgements about people, events, and things is essential for effective functioning in the world. Problems arise when we start believing and acting as if our judgements are facts rather than subjective opinions.

When I judge you, the benefit you get is an insight into my particular way of perceiving things. You learn nothing about yourself because, given the identical set of circumstances, your judgement may be entirely different than mine, based on your particular perspectives, experiences, and mental models. Judging others helps us to discover what we believe. We learn about our own perceptions of the world.

In considering our judgements, it is critical to recognize that when we judge others what we are actually doing is assessing their behaviour against our own mental models. The only legitimate benefit we gain from our judgements is a better understanding of the mental models we are operating under.

The insights our judgements provide us are not an accurate assessment of people, events, and things but more an accurate understanding of our own values, beliefs, assumptions, and mental models. When we judge another person negatively for something they did, we learn that if we were to behave the same way, we would judge ourselves as we are judging this person. If a particular response triggers a negative judgement, then the opposite response must be what we value. So what we are telling ourselves is that if we faced a similar situation, we would respond the opposite way to how this person responded.

As we become aware that our judgements contain valuable information about our own values, beliefs, and mental models, we discover that the Universe is constantly presenting us with opportunities to discover who we truly are. Through careful observation we get a more accurate picture of how we perceive the world and begin to see how they influence our behaviour. Identifying and discovering what our judgements are telling us about ourselves enables us to understand what we actually believe and value. Greater understanding helps us respond more authentically and effectively.

To become more authentic and effective we need to do two things the moment we realize we're making a judgement. First, we need to acknowledge that our judgement is the result of our particular worldview and not an objective reflection of the thing being judged. Second, we need to ask ourselves the following questions.

- What am I telling me about me based on my judgement of this situation?

- What are my underlying beliefs, values, assumptions, and mental models that support this judgement?

- Now that I understand the reason for this judgement, what have I learned about how strongly I believe what I believe, and about how I prefer to respond if faced with a similar situation?

This is the goldmine of personal insight that our judgements invite us to uncover. Self-awareness is the benefit we gain from identifying what we truly value and believe. This process of self-examination is key to our growth, wisdom, and maturity.

The next time you believe your judgement of someone or something to be about them, think again. And the next time you're on the receiving end of someone else's judgement, remember that not only is their judgement of you *not* about you, their judgement has just provided you with a window into *their* worldview. The opportunity is to let their judgement of you flow right on by (unless it is something you believe might be helpful for your growth) and to ask yourself the following questions.

- What am I learning about this person based on the thought-system that has them judging this situation the way they do?

- Does their judgement have merit?

- Is their perspective sufficiently insightful or interesting that it warrants further investigation and discussion?

If their judgement runs contrary to yours and holds no appeal for you, then by that judgement you have validated your perspective. When we encounter contrary judgements we are presented with a great opportunity.

- If I don't believe or support this judgement, then what do I believe?

- Am I acting in alignment with my belief?

- What would acting in alignment with this belief look like in concrete terms (how would I act when faced with a similar situation)?

Keep in mind that many of our judgements change over time. That being the case, the wise person resists the temptation to become rigid in their judgements lest they miss an insight or opportunity to learn, grow, and evolve. Both experience and wisdom teach us to resist the temptation of stubbornly asserting that *our* truth is *the* truth.

So much suffering in the world could be avoided if people had a little more humility to acknowledge that they don't have a monopoly on "the truth." If only we were all a little more willing to keep an open mind when encountering different opinions, perceptions and beliefs than our own. It's not that our perspectives need to blow whichever way the wind blows, but by holding our "truths" lightly we remain open, willing, and interested in life-long learning. The colour and richness of the universe promises the open-minded seeker an endless stream of wonders so long as we continue to own our judgements and constantly subject them to compassionate investigation while maintaining those that support our growth and gracefully releasing those that no longer reflect the person we have become.

One test I use to determine if my judgements are effective or ineffective is to ask myself: "Does this opinion, belief, or perception support my ability to encounter and extend unconditional love in my life and the lives of everyone I touch, or is it fear-based and obstructive to my ability to live in harmony with my own loving nature?"

May you stay forever curious about what your judgements are telling you about you.

EXPANDING SELF-AWARENESS

1. Am I beginning to recognize that projecting my judgements onto the world, rather than owning them myself, prevents me from learning more about me?

2. Can I see how my judgements of people, things, and situations have value to the extent that they help me discover what I value and appreciate?

3. Based on the negative judgements I have about people, things, and situations, what am I discovering I value and appreciate through identifying the positive opposites of the things I reject?

4. How effectively am I living these positive opposites?

5. How willing am I to hold my judgements lightly knowing that they may change as new information becomes available?

APPLYING SELF-AWARENESS

Take a sheet of paper and draw a line down the middle of the page. On the left hand top of the page write: "Positive Judgements." On the right hand top of the page write: "Negative Judgements." For a few minutes, reflect on and note the people, things, and situations that you value, appreciate, and believe positively impact the world. Then reflect on and note the people, things, and situations that you don't respect or appreciate, and believe negatively impact the world. After identifying as many positive and negative judgements as you can, ask yourself the following questions.

1. Looking at my positive judgements, what do I believe positively contributes to the quality of life for others and me?

2. Looking at my negative judgements, what do I believe undermines the quality of life for others and me?

3. What are the positive opposites of my negative judgements?

4. What am I discovering I want more of in my life and in the world?

5. What emotions come up for me from this exercise?

6. Based on what I learned, what—if anything—will I change?

7. What do I hope these changes will do to improve the quality of my life?

CHAPTER SEVEN:

TRUST YOUR BODY

One of the things I've discovered over the years is that every time I make a decision that compromises my values, I register that compromise in my body. When I act honourably (as defined by my own value system), my body feels relaxed and open. When I act in ways that violate my value system, I feel my body tightening up as though it is trying to protect itself. After reviewing as many incidents as I could remember, I discovered a predictable relationship between my choices and the way my body experiences them.

It turns out that our body accurately reflects the relationship between our actions and our values. This is a useful discovery because while we can be tricked by our thinking into doing things that make logical sense but actually harm others or ourselves, our body is never fooled. Our body is like an independent observer who simply identifies when we are acting in alignment with, or contrary to, our values. It provides experiential evidence to communicate that fact to us.

As I became more conscious of this experiential information coming from my body, I wondered if I could use it when the situation got trickier, when it was hard to know if I was honouring or violating my deepest values.

One such occasion to test this question occurred when I was working with a group of people and a woman began chatting with me. In short order, she got very intense discussing her worldview and how similar she thought her view was to mine. While there were similarities, I wasn't at all sure we were as similar as she seemed to think. At one point she invited me to stay with her and her boyfriend at property they owned on a resort island. She was quite insistent that I make a commitment to visit. As she was pressing the invitation on me, I realized that my mind was having trouble deciding how to respond. Was this something I wanted to do? Did I need time to think about it? As these questions popped into my head, I realized that I simply didn't have enough information about her, or her invitation, to make an informed decision.

While this internal dialogue was going on, I realized that my body was reacting quite powerfully. As I focused my attention inwards, I became aware that my body was moving into a protective mode. I felt myself contracting. My body wanted to get away from this woman. My body's reaction informed me that, for whatever reason, I was uncomfortable with her invitation. I made the decision in that moment to not pursue the conversation further. I made a polite exit, and my body immediately began to relax.

On another occasion I was having a conversation with a friend when a stranger approached and started telling us his tale of woes. He was visibly upset, and as he shared his story he started crying. In my mind I was thinking, "Okay, buddy, I know you want me to give you some money, so just ask me for it so I can continue talking with my friend." Eventually he did ask for money, and acting out of simple compassion I gave him some and he walked away. I turned to my friend to continue our conversation and she immediately stopped me and said, "Oh no. You're not going to just carry on our conversation without acknowledging what just took place."

At first I didn't understand what she was meant. My mind had already moved on, and I wasn't interested in revisiting what just took place. But since this is a very wise friend, and her challenge had a loving intention, I decided to follow her lead. She asked me to examine my motives in giving this man money. I responded that he was in rough shape and I didn't mind giving him a few bucks. She pushed back. "What was your real motivation for giving him money?" As I thought back I became aware that while he was talking my body was getting more and more agitated. His sad story and his tears were really bugging me, and as he continued talking I continued to feel tighter and tighter inside. I realized that my motivation for giving him money was to get rid of him and relieve my discomfort. Compassion played no part in my decision.

This was a very important insight and key learning for me. It confirmed that my body was providing me with accurate information on my actual state of being, even as my brain was telling me something completely different. If my friend hadn't insisted that I reflect on the situation, I would have concluded that my actions were motivated by compassion and gener-osity. In reality, my actions were motivated by my desire to get this fellow out of my face as quickly as possible. I paid him to go away.

What I love about this learning is the fact that I was able to get a more accurate understanding of the forces that govern my behaviour. I had no judgement about my choice; rather, I valued being able to see my real intentions more clearly. Compassionate inquiry is really important, in situa-tions like this, to teach us more about ourselves. When we judge ourselves, our ego feels threatened and we lose the ability to follow our thinking back to the source.

The purpose of learning to listen to our body, and of comparing what it's telling us to what our mind is suggesting, is to discover our real inten-tions. This discovery helps identify our real motivations. When faced with a similar situation in the future, what—if anything—might we do differently? This process of self-discovery is essential if we are to gain greater insights into the responses we make and our underlying motivations. As the ability to correctly interpret deeper motives by listening to our body improves, our ability to consciously make more effective and value-based choices and decisions improves as well.

ATTRACTION AND REPULSION

In light of the growing awareness that our body produces physical reactions in response to our inner and outer world, the question becomes: "How can I use this information from my body to help me make more effective choices?" Also: "What else can I learn from the wisdom of my body?"

The information our body communicates not only informs us when we are making life-enhancing and life-diminishing choices, it also provides us with insights into our values and true nature. Let me demonstrate how this works through a simple exercise.

EXPERIENTIAL EXERCISE

Sitting in a comfortable position, take a couple of deep breaths. Let your body relax. Now think about a time when you were deeply happy. Perhaps it was when you held a sleeping baby, with their wonderful baby smell and their warm little body moulded into yours. Perhaps you were listening to a great piece of music or doing something with a close friend. Perhaps it was something else that brings you an experience of deep happiness. Visualize that event as clearly as you can, and notice how your body is feeling in the moment.

- Are you aware of how open and relaxed your body is feeling?

- Can you sense the ease of your breath and the calm pace of your heartbeat?

- Can you sense your body's openness, relaxation, and deep calm?

Spend a minute noticing how your body is informing you of how it experiences safety. Try this short exercise with any memory and see if you can detect a consistent pattern within your body.

The degree of physical reaction is directly proportional to the intensity of the emotion, so a modest recollection of joy or happiness will generate a modest response from your body. It isn't particularly excited or powerfully moved; instead it feels light and calm. No stress, no great waves of energy moving through you, just a quiet calm and a generally peaceful condition.

More profound or powerful memories generate more profound or powerful physical reactions such as a strong wave of energy moving through you, deepened or rapid breathing, or a faster heart rate. Your body might tingle, and you may experience a sense of euphoria, as though you could float off the ground from feeling so alive, so happy, so grateful. Can you sense how your body reacts when powerful, positive emotions move through you?

Now let's explore how your body reacts to negative events. Take a couple of deep breaths and think about a particularly undesirable event in your life—a time when you were frustrated, irritated, frightened, or angry. Maybe someone cut you off in traffic. Perhaps you got into an argument with someone and you got increasingly angry. Perhaps you were around someone you didn't feel safe with, or something really scared you. Now, pay attention to how your body is reacting.

- Can you feel it tightening up?

- Are your hands beginning to clench?

- Are your shoulders getting tight?

- What is happening to your breathing? Is it getting shallower and more rapid?

- Can you feel your heart speeding up?

As with our positive emotions, the intensity of our body's reaction is proportional to the intensity of the negative experience. Minor irritants are barely noticeable at the body level while powerful encounters with fear, anger, and intense stress produce powerful responses in our body. Have you ever found yourself tossing and turning in the night—your body sweating, your heart pounding over something particularly threatening? Are you ever up late worrying about what is occurring in your life? Can you detect the pattern of how your body reacts when faced with varying degrees of negative emotions?

Understanding how your body reacts when facing different kinds of emotions, from ecstatic joy to terror and everything in between, is a powerful way to discover how your body communicates with you and provides you with an alternative method of recognizing the safety or danger of any situation or condition you're in at a particular moment in time. While our minds can be tricked and manipulated, our body is not fooled by clever arguments. Can you think of a time when you met someone and, even though they were doing and saying all the right things, you had a gut feeling that they couldn't be trusted? That gut feeling is your body's way of informing you that you don't feel safe. Your mind might not be able to identify the nature of the threat, but your body is sending you a clear signal: something isn't safe here and you should re-evaluate this situation as quickly as possible.

As you become more familiar and consciously aware of the way your body responds to different situations, you will quickly begin to recognize when you feel safe, happy, grateful, joyful, fearful, angry, frustrated, etc. based on your body's predictable reactions to situations.

So how can we use the wisdom of our body to make more effective choices in our life? One of the ways is to compare what we think about a given situation with how our body is reacting to it. Regardless of the situation we find ourselves in, we can check in with our body to see what it is telling us. Ask yourself the following questions.

- Do I feel safe?

- Do I feel uncomfortable?

- Is this person or situation stimulating a physical reaction of openness, warmth, and expansion or a reaction of danger and self-protection?

Answers to these questions are useful in guiding our responses. By paying attention to what our body is telling us, we can either move to engage in or remove ourselves from a situation based on how our body is reacting. For example, I might find myself at a social function where there is a lot of drinking going on. Perhaps for the first few hours I feel comfortable. Later on, I begin to notice that I'm getting irritated. My body is starting to tighten up; perhaps I'm starting to feel restless. This is my body's way of telling me that something about this situation has changed and I would be wise to leave this environment.

Perhaps you're having a conversation with someone that at first may be interesting or at least neutral, but as the conversation progresses you become aware that your body is becoming more and more uncomfortable. This person is becoming more insistent or more aggressive in their delivery, and you no longer feel safe whether intellectually, because he's trying to convince you of his position and expecting you to agree with him, or physically, because his body language is becoming more aggressive and it's starting to feel like a confrontation which you have no desire to partake in. Your body is letting you know that you no longer feel comfortable with this interaction. As long as you stay or until something changes, the feeling is going to grow.

When you become aware that your body is communicating with you, it is very important not to be judgemental but to become attentive and curious. Your most resourceful and effective response is to simply observe and acknowledge what is going on inside and to let that information inform you about how you're experiencing the situation. The way your body is responding is not about the situation. It's about how you're *interpreting* the situation. For whatever reason, your body is informing you that you're not feeling safe in the situation you're in, and it would be wise to remove yourself. Later on, you can reflect on what triggered your body's reaction. A good time to reflect and investigate yourself is once you're feeling safe again. Ask yourself the following questions.

- What was going on that generated the feeling of irritation, risk, or danger?

- What did I feel repelled by?

Gaining greater awareness of our body signals benefits us in two ways. First, we discover the people, places, and things that we are attracted to. Those things and events that our body indicates generate feelings of being alive, happy, joyful, etc. Second, we discover those things we are repelled by—those people, places, and things that generate feelings of danger, risk, self-protection, etc. It's important to note that these bodily reactions are not always an accurate indicator of *real* danger in any situation. For example, I may be feeling self-protective even when there is no objective danger. What my body is telling me, notwithstanding any actual danger, is that it feels threatened. I have learned to honour my body's messages and to reflect later on to discover more about my own perceptions, feelings, and beliefs of the particular person, place or thing that triggered my body's defensive reaction.

The things we are attracted to reflect our values, beliefs, and desires. The things we are repelled by identify what we don't value, believe, or desire. Most importantly, our body helps us understand the story we're telling ourselves about ourselves. Let me illustrate how this understanding supports our positive development.

As noted in chapter six, our judgements of the world tell us nothing about the world; they only tell us about ourselves. The things we are attracted to and repelled by inform us about the mental models we have regarding particular people, places, and events. As I become conscious of the things I am attracted to and repelled by, I can ask myself:

- How did I come to hold a favourable or unfavourable judgement about this person, place, or event?

- What value, belief, or desire is being reinforced or undermined by this particular person, place, or event?

- Do I have any evidence that my judgement might be inaccurate?

- If I suspect it may be inaccurate, what am I willing to do to investigate or test my conclusion?

This kind of self-scrutiny is how we stay open to continuously evaluating our judgements so we can discover which serve us and which need to be revised or replaced in order for us to grow.

When you have a reaction to a person, place, or event—whether positive or negative—you gain a useful piece of information about your own perceptions, feelings, and beliefs triggered by the situation. When you are attracted to someone's presence or conversation, what you learn is that there are things the two of you share in common. There is an alignment between your perceptions, feelings, or beliefs. Equally informative: when you are repelled by someone, this informs you that you have different perceptions, feelings, or beliefs. In both cases, you learn about the assumptions and mental models you're holding inside by observing your reaction to the outside world.

I cannot overstate the powerful benefits that arise from recognizing that what we are attracted to and repelled by is all about our perceptions, feelings, and beliefs. It tells us very little about the outside world other than which parts align or conflict with our assumptions and mental models. Owning our judgements of the world is a critical step towards understanding ourselves better. Once we know how we view the world, we can evaluate our judgements. Are they improving or undermining our quality of life? Then we can decide if we want to maintain, revise, or replace a particular assumption or model.

Let me give you a personal example to illustrate how truly beneficial this process is.

I was sitting at an outside café enjoying a cup of coffee when a casual acquaintance approached me and asked if he could sit down. He began engaging in small talk about his family and other things and then began to share some of his experiences about his younger years. Without preamble, he started telling me about his involvement in the neo-Nazi movement and his opinions about visible minorities. I immediately had a powerful negative reaction to this conversation and was aware that I was disgusted by what he was saying. I had no desire to engage him in a debate; I wanted to get as far away from him as I could. Really upset by his bigotry, I made an excuse to leave. Depression over centuries of human suffering, and anger at the ignorance of intolerance and the cruelty of blind hatred flooded my emotions and filled me with profound sadness. "Why do people have to think this way? Is it ever going to change? What, if anything, can I do about it?" On and on, these questions tore across my mind as I walked home.

After a considerable length of time, I settled down and called a friend to share my experience. After listening to my story he said:

"So what you're saying is that you feel really strongly about seeing past people's skin colour or religion. That judging people by how they look or where they were born or the God they worship doesn't reflect how you judge people. In fact, what I hear you saying is that everything this guy said is a direct contradiction to your deeply held beliefs about people's right to be respected as equal human beings. Have I got it right?"

"Yes," I said, "that pretty much sums up my position."

"Great," he said. "Then by the same standard of equality, you believe this guy too should be regarded as equal, even though you completely disagree with his view of visible minorities, etc. Right?" He paused. "In fact, you really owe him a debt of gratitude for helping you discover just how powerfully you feel about this."

As hard as it was to hear what he was saying, I could find no fault in his logic. I had to acknowledge that the neo-Nazi had triggered some powerful emotions in me, and that by understanding what I was rejecting in his worldview, I simultaneously confirmed the intensity of my own position on this subject. This was a very powerful, difficult, and effective lesson for me about owning my judgements. I discovered more about myself by analyzing what I found to be reprehensible and then identifying what I actually believed. This experience taught me just how important my value of human equality really is, based on the strength of my reaction when that belief was confronted by an opposite opinion. Being repelled by this fellow wasn't actually about him, it was about me. The intensity of my reaction to his opinions confirmed just how strongly I felt (and still do).

This experience taught me that understanding what we are attracted to and repelled by is not always pleasant or easy, but if we have the patience to take ourselves to a calm, reflective place to investigate what we're telling ourselves about ourselves, based on our reactions to outside situations we can learn a great deal. From there, we can decide what—if anything—we want to do with that knowledge to more effectively reflect our worldview.

Let me share another experience, of the opposite kind, to illustrate how the things we are attracted to can help us release a harmful mental model and replace it with a more effective and life-enhancing one.

I was having a visit with a very dear friend. I trust her completely and know, in the core of my being, that whatever she says or does, her deepest intention is unconditional love. As we were standing in my living room talking about something she turned to me, put her arms on my shoulders, and with tears streaming down her face said: "If someone who loves you as much as I love you can't get through your defences, then how are you ever going to be able to experience love?" Instantly my body reacted with fear. It was letting me know, in no uncertain terms, that this was a very dangerous situation that I should escape from as quickly as possible. But there was a problem. While my body was giving me completely accurate information about the emotional danger of this situation, I was also deeply attracted to her message because, while the situation felt threatening, the person delivering the message was someone I loved and trusted completely, and her only motivation was to help me.

Knowing that something potentially threatening yet beneficial was happening, I decided to lean into my discomfort and encouraged her to carry on. As I quizzed her about her comments, I became aware that my body was starting to settle into a more peaceful place, and her words were beginning to penetrate.

As she talked I realized that she had identified my fear of vulnerability. At some point in my life I developed a mental model that being vulnerable produced pain and was something to be avoided at all costs. While this model did provide me some measure of emotional safety, it also brought the unintended consequence of preventing me from receiving emotional love from others. My decision to keep myself safe had effectively cut me off from the love that people were trying to offer me and prevented them from having a deeper and more intimate connection with me.

My friend was calling me out on this defensive coping strategy and letting me know that the barrier I had erected out of fear of being emotionally hurt was preventing her—and others—from having a more intimate relationship with me. By looking deep within I realized she was absolutely right and I made the decision to release this ineffective mental model so I could experience greater connection and learn how to live more intimately and authentically.

By no means, has this choice been quick and easy. I am still working on it to this day. The real benefit of releasing this out-dated mental model is my ability to experience and express more tenderness, intimacy, and love in my relationships with others. Since that conversation took place, I've experienced more love, joy, and genuine happiness in my relationships with others than I had experienced in the preceding 50 years.

As a general rule, when my body tells me someone is coming from a condemning or unloving place, I ignore what they have to say even if the information they're giving me may have some merit. The fact that they're coming from an unloving place, as determined by how my body reacts to them, enables me to simply tune them out. I don't get concerned about losing the benefit of the information they possess. I long ago discovered that the information I need to grow and mature is presented by multiple people and situations. On the other hand, when I recognize that someone is coming from a loving place, then even if their words are difficult to hear, I do my best to stay open to them. Our Higher Power speaks to us through loving people. These people frequently play the role of spiritual guides in helping us towards a deeper understanding of any error traps or unhealthy mental models we are holding. Through the loving assistance of others we can compassionately release error traps and unhealthy mental models to improve the quality of our own lives and, by extension, the lives of everyone we touch.

Our goal is greater self-understanding. The way to maximize this outcome is to stay safe while we explore what we are attracted to and repelled by. Try to stay compassionate and unconditionally accepting with yourself, regardless of where your exploration takes you. Remember that everything you've ever done made perfect sense at the time. While it may no longer be serving you, it began as an attempt by your ego to bring you genuine happiness and to reduce your suffering. Acknowledge that fact, be grateful for your ego's efforts on your behalf, and gently release those error traps and mental models that are no longer serving you so you can make room for more effective models.

EXPANDING SELF-AWARENESS

1. What does my body feel like with I am acting in alignment with my values?

2. What does my body feel like with I am acting contrary to my values?

3. Do I recognize that my mind can get confused, but my body always knows the truth?

4. Do I honour my body's messages?

5. What can I start doing today to hear and positively respond to what my body is trying to tell me?

APPLYING SELF-AWARENESS

Take a sheet of paper and draw a line down the middle of the page. On the left hand top of the page write: "Things my body feels attracted to." On the right hand top of the page write: "Things my body feels repelled by." After identifying as many people, places, and events you can think of that you are attracted to and repelled by, ask yourself the following questions.

1. What qualities and characteristics does my body feel attracted to?

2. What characteristics does my body feel repelled by?

3. What is my body telling me I want more of?

4. What is my body telling me I want to avoid?

5. What emotions come up for me from this exercise?

6. Based on what I learned, what—if anything—will I change?

7. What do I hope these changes will do to improve the quality of my life?

CHAPTER EIGHT:

WE ARE ABSOLUTELY AND EXCLUSIVELY RESPONSIBLE FOR EVERY EXPERIENCE WE HAVE

Our interpretations create our reality. It is our thoughts, perceptions, and behaviours that create and determine our life-situation and our experience, not the other way around. Thoughts have a way of becoming facts in our life. Suppose someone has the thought: "I am a lousy public speaker. Every time I try to speak in public I start to panic. My palms begin to sweat, my mouth goes dry, and my knees begin to shake uncontrollably at which point I completely forget what I wanted to say and fight the urge to bolt from the stage before I make an even bigger fool of myself." As long as we hold onto these thoughts, we will experience the undesirable outcomes imagined. And when our worst fears actually occur, we tell ourselves: "You see, I was right. I told you I was a lousy public speaker. I'm never going to do that again." This is the nature of a self-fulfilling prophecy.

Another thing we need to recognize about perceptions is that we see what we focus on. Take the following examples.

Perception: People have an incredible capacity to rise above their hardships.

Validation: I turn on the TV and see a documentary on Mother Teresa winning the Nobel Peace Prize for her humanitarian work in the slums of Calcutta. I'm sitting in the doctor's office and I pick up an old copy of Reader's Digest to find an article on Helen Keller who wrote several books in spite of being blind, deaf, and mute. I pick up a newspaper and read about the annual Terry Fox run that has raised over $300 million for cancer research and is still going strong 21 years after his death.

Perception: People are basically dishonest and given half a chance will rob you blind.

Validation: I turn on the TV and observe CEOs of fortune 500 companies, accused of defrauding millions from their shareholders, being escorted in handcuffs from their penthouse offices. I read about a home invasion where an elderly couple were tied up and beaten half to death; the thieves stole a television worth $450; the husband is in a coma and is not expected to live.

Perceptions of incredible capacity and profound dishonesty were both validated by information found in the world. Our perception determines what we focus on and how we experience our lives.

Whatever we focus on is reflected back at us. When we focus on pain, anger, and injustice, these are the aspects of reality we notice, and it confirms our opinions. When we focus on compassion, courage, and justice, these qualities are what we notice.

We always retain the power to choose what we focus on—the problems or the solutions, the light or the dark, the noble or the despicable, faith or fear, love or hate, constructive or destructive, positive or negative, wealth or poverty, abundance or scarcity, the choice is always and exclusively ours. No one outside of us is ultimately responsible for the life we're experiencing or our life-situation, which is the result of our thoughts about the world and the things we choose to focus on.

This can be a difficult idea to accept particularly when we remember things that were done to us by others—through no fault of our own—that were painful, unfair, and undeserved.

"How is it possible to accept responsibility for those things over which we are completely powerless to do anything about?"

It's true that there are events that happen over which you have no control. What you do have control over, in all situations, is the way you choose to interpret them and how you choose to respond. Your perception of the event, not the event itself, determines your experiences and shapes your responses to it.

Some people, when confronted with incredibly difficult circumstances, decide that there is nothing they can do about it and descend into self-pity and self-destructive behaviour. Other people, faced with equally difficult circumstances, decide that they will not be overwhelmed and make choices that allow them to transcend their difficulties. Often, they discover insights and abilities unknown to them before their difficulties arose.

Two young athletic men were riding in the back of separate pick-up trucks. Both were thrown from the trucks and both broke their necks. Both become paraplegics. One became so depressed that he died within a few months of the accident. The other young man chose to respond differently to his condition. He decided to raise public awareness about people with spinal cord injuries. To accomplish this, he decided to push his wheelchair around the world.

Few people remember the name of the young man who died of depression, and most would say that it wasn't his fault, that tragic circumstances were to blame. But the more painful truth is that his thoughts, perceptions, and responses to his situation were a contributing factor in his death. He died because he believed his situation was hopeless. His thoughts influenced his perceptions and behaviours, which reflected his "truth" ("*My life is over.*") and his life progressed the only way it could for someone who held the thoughts he did about his situation.

The other man, Rick Hansen, became an international ambassador for spinal cord research. When we look at the choices Rick made in response to his situation, we can see how his thoughts produced behaviours that ultimately expanded his influence, raised millions of dollars, stimulated research, and motivated countless others to rise above their perceived limitations and embrace life with courage, determination, and purpose.

Both men suffered terrible injuries, and each experienced the natural consequences of his thoughts, perceptions, and behaviours based on how he chose to interpret his situation. I am not judging the choices, I am merely pointing out that our choices arise from how we choose to interpret the circumstances we encounter, and our responses to these interpretations produce natural and logical consequences.

To say that each of us is ultimately responsible for the life we have because of the thoughts, perceptions, and beliefs we're holding is not to be insensitive to the suffering we have experienced. Each of us has experienced unearned suffering, and each of us has caused unearned suffering. Neither of these conditions prevents us from accepting responsibility for the fact that in every instance it is *we* who apply the meaning to the circumstances we encounter and, from that interpretation, decide how we will respond. As Leslie (1969) noted, "Over and above all conditioning influences, man's life unfolds as he exercises his freedom to make conscious decisions" (p. 21). When we stop blaming others and realize that our thoughts, perceptions, and behaviours are creating the life we are experiencing, then we have found the key to changing our experience. To get a different experience, we need to change our interpretation of the situation. The path to this unlimited power and potential, to create an entirely new experience, is found in three simple words. "*I am responsible.*"

When we see ourselves at the mercy of others, then powerlessness, fear, and depression dominate our life. When we recognize we have the power to let go of our resentments and justified anger by changing the way we view past events—because our current views are no longer serving us—then we create an opportunity to reframe how we perceive events, and that reframe changes the impact of past conditions and future responses. Revising our responses changes our experience and our life-situation.

A simple example of this is when someone gets injured and has to reduce their workload until they recover. If that person happens to live a frantic existence, this event represents a huge challenge and, on first inspection, a tremendous burden. But suppose the forced time away from work happens to awaken them to the realization that their frantic pace has resulted in them neglecting important areas of their life that they were previously too busy to notice. Their injury provided the interruption they needed to realize how unbalanced their life had become. In hindsight, their injury may have been the best thing that ever happened to them.

In being willing to view the situations we encounter from multiple perspectives, we frequently discover hidden gifts of insight and awareness that were there all along but which we couldn't see because we were so focused on one particular facet of our life. By changing our perspective, we change our experience. Circumstances in and of themselves do not determine our experience, our interpretations and behaviours about them does.

I don't mind confessing that I found it a real challenge to accept that the experiences I was having didn't actually arise from my circumstances but from the way I interpreted them. My biggest personal challenge was the realization that if this was true, then the burden of responsibility for my experiences was entirely my own and no one else's. The upside is that I don't need anyone else to change in order to have a more satisfying experience. The downside is that I can no longer blame others for the experience I'm having. If I want to improve my experiences, I need to reframe my circumstances.

This concept of personal responsibility for my experiences contradicted my long-held belief that other people were at least partially responsible for my experiences. I reasoned that I might start out being happy until someone said or did something that upset me. Obviously it *had* to be them who caused my feelings to change because I was feeling fine until they said or did something to change my experience. As reasonable and logical as this conclusion appears to be, like so many other beliefs, I eventually came to understand that this too was an error trap that I needed to replace.

I can recall the first time I clearly understood the role I played in creating my own experience. It was a warm, sunny afternoon at an outside café drinking coffee with a couple of female friends. I was in a very peaceful mood and was enjoying the conversation and the day. At some point one of them started talking about how, in her opinion, all men are pigs. For the next 20 minutes she proceeded to tell me how men couldn't be trusted, that they were basically predators and even those who weren't predators were untrustworthy. As the only representative of my gender at the table, it was hard for me not to feel that her comments were being directed at me, and that I should say something to challenge her assertions. I was also aware that all the while she was railing against men, she was staring directly at me and didn't seem to register that if her accusations were accurate, then by implication I too must be a predator who could never be trusted. I wondered how she was able to ignore the glaring contradiction that she was pouring out her heart to the very object of her contempt, and yet she didn't seem to notice that fact.

While some part of my consciousness was thinking that I should be feeling pretty upset by this blanket accusation being levelled against all men, I was also aware that she really needed to get this anger off her chest. I found myself in a remarkably peaceful space. Rather than feeling the need to defend my gender, I found myself being deeply aware that the most effective response I could make was to simply be a conscious witness as she unloaded her pain, anger, and fear. I remember a psychologist once remarking that anger is one way people express their emotional pain. I also realized, on some level of consciousness, that my compassionate and empathetic response was the most compelling counter-argument to her criticisms, and that the mere act of silently witnessing her tirade brought into question her negative worldview about men. Not that I believed for one minute that this contradiction would penetrate her consciousness.

As I sat there, the other woman sitting with us became increasingly agitated and at one point began defending the integrity and trustworthiness of the men she knew. She argued that in her experience she had met numerous men who had consistently treated her with courtesy, dignity, and respect. In her opinion, the conclusions the first woman was drawing against all men wasn't accurate or fair. This assault and defence of men carried on until the woman expelling her fear and pain finally ran out of gas and stopped talking.

What I was aware of was that, quite to my surprise, I continued to feel incredibly peaceful and relaxed. It was something of a wonder to observe my interior experience throughout her critical monologue and to discover that at no point did I get sucked into her experience. I managed to remain calm and peaceful while intuitively knowing that the most loving thing I could do was to give this wounded woman a safe forum to vent.

Once she left the table, the other woman expressed her regret that I was on the receiving end of such a hostile attack on men. She wanted me to know that she completely rejected the first woman's position, and expressed her deep appreciation for our friendship and the respect she felt for me. She asked me if I was okay, and I responded that in fact I was feeling completely peaceful and relaxed, and had somehow been feeling it more and more as the monologue built to its eventual conclusion. I explained that somewhere inside me I knew that this tirade had nothing to do with me personally and that the greatest act of friendship I could offer this raging woman was to simply witness her anger and fear so she wouldn't continue holding it inside her. I assured the second woman that I was unharmed by the experience. She reiterated her love and respect for me and then left the table.

As I sat there reflecting on the extraordinary event that had just trans-pired, I began to examine how it had been possible for me not to react to the first woman's verbal assault against men. Some part of my brain was telling me that I should have been upset by her words—she was looking directly at me the whole time she was tearing into the integrity, dignity, and honour of men. I could see how easily it would have been for me to become angry, defensive, or aggressive in the face of such naked aggression, yet I was aware that none of these reactions ever surfaced. How was this possible? How had I been able to remain calm and peaceful, choosing the role of a witness rather than the accused needing to defend the honour of his kind?

It occurred to me that the reason I was able to stay in a peaceful space was because of the way I chose to interpret the situation. Rather than choosing to define it as an assault on me and other men, I chose to define it as a deep pain needing escape from the confines of this woman's body and mind. As it turned out, my response wasn't particularly helpful because the more she talked, the angrier she got. When she finally ran out of gas, she was more upset than when she began. But from my perspective, it worked because the angrier she got, the calmer I became. It was as if the clarity of my interpretation enabled me to increase my calm in direct proportion to her hostility.

This encounter taught me, in the clearest possible terms, that my experience is not determined by the situation I find myself in but rather by how I choose to interpret it. It truly is our interpretation that determines our experience.

Following this encounter I began testing this theory in a variety of situations and conditions. Being cut off in my car, dealing with rush hour traffic, listening to people expound thoughts and ideas I completely rejected, being in social situations where I wasn't enjoying myself. In every case, when I became aware of how I was feeling, by consciously choosing to reframe my interpretation of what was going on I immediately got a new experience. The practical lesson I learned from my encounter with this suffering, angry woman was that each of us possesses the power to determine our experience by choosing how we interpret external events.

Our ability to reframe our interpretation of situations and conditions is an amazing gift since it frees us from having to change others in order to be happy. We can't change anyone without their cooperation, so to depend on others to change before we can be happy is to hold ourselves hostage to the conditions of others. When they treat us well, we're happy, and when they treat us badly, we suffer. This is how I believed things worked for many years. I am forever grateful to finally realize that it is within ourselves and not from others that the power to determine our experience resides. It is we, not others, who are responsible and empowered to choose how we interpret the situations we encounter and, through our interpretations, determine the experience we have. When we decide that we don't like the experience we're having, we are free to reinterpret the situation in such a way as to create a different experience for ourselves. It is the meaning we attach to the behaviours of the outside world that creates our experience, not the outside world itself. Therein lies our power to change our experiences.

We, and no one else, are absolutely and exclusively responsible for our experiences since we alone have the power to change our experience the moment we choose to interpret them differently.

Now, you might be wondering whether this strategy is nothing more than some fancy mental smoke and mirrors that allows others to treat us badly and for us to simply take it by changing our interpretation of their abusive treatment towards us. Nothing could be farther from the truth. Even in our suffering we have the capacity to convert our pain into an effective instrument for growth. Consider the suffering Victor Frankl endured in the concentration camp. Consider the injustice imposed on the countless individuals struggling for their civil rights. Martin Luther King once remarked that: "unearned suffering is redemptive." While you may not agree with his opinion, what you can observe is that by choosing to interpret their suffering as redemptive, people in the civil rights movement were able to remain resourceful and committed rather than bitter and hostile. Eventually they won the justice they were seeking without resorting to violence and bloodshed. It was, in no small measure, their moral authority arising from their non-violent response to naked aggression that shifted the tide of public opinion in their favour.

As we begin to understand that the power to determine our experience lies within us, the next step is to review the blame we've placed on others for our unhappiness and then identify our role in maintaining it. We can continue to blame others and get the corresponding experience of frustration and powerlessness, or we can choose to reframe the situation to get a more positive experience. I used to blame everybody else for the struggles I was having until I realized that the only common denominator among all my struggles was how I was choosing to interpret and respond to them. By letting go of blame and accepting responsibility for the interpretations I was making, I recognized that as long as I kept trying to get a better experience by changing others, nothing was going to improve. It was only when I became willing to let go of my judgements and accepted responsibility for how I was interpreting the situation that I was able to change my experience. As my experiences improved, my behaviour became more constructive and the quality of my life dramatically improved.

One of the most powerful perceptions that assault our experience is the mentally generated fear of things that have yet to come. These projected fears can trigger fantastic anxiety as we attempt to find solutions to these imaginary worst-case scenarios. Our goal in the next chapter is to take a closer look at our fears so we can distinguish the legitimate life-saving fear responses from the far more common imaginary fears that suck mental energy away from us and distort our perceptions and feelings of safety and appreciation for the life we actually have.

EXPANDING SELF-AWARENESS

1. Knowing that my interpretations create my experience through a self-fulfilling prophecy, what interpretations—if any—am I willing to reconsider to get a different experience?

2. Knowing that what we focus on expands, and we always retain the power to choose what we focus on, what am I choosing to focus on?

3. When have I judged something negatively that ultimately proved to be a blessing in disguise?

4. How do my expectations of others change knowing that I am absolutely and exclusively responsible for my experience?

5. What event can I reinterpret to convert unearned suffering into redemptive healing?

APPLYING SELF-AWARENESS

On a sheet of paper, write about a current person or situation you are unsatisfied with and then answer the following questions.

1. Who do I hold responsible for my experiences?

2. What do I believe they need to change in order for me to feel better?

3. What is the risk of holding others responsible for my happiness?

4. If I accept that I am absolutely and exclusively responsible for the experience I am having, how can I look at this person or situation differently to get a more satisfying experience?

5. What emotions come up for me from this exercise?

6. Based on what I learned, what—if anything—will I change?

7. What do I hope these changes will do to improve the quality of my life?

CHAPTER NINE:

FALSE EVIDENCE APPEARING REAL (FEAR)

There are three distinct kinds of fear that impact the quality of our life. The first is the fear when encountering a bear on the trail, or an angry dog that's broken its leash and is running towards you. This fear is the highly desirable and very effective survival reaction of our old brain trying to keep us safe. The second kind of fear is undesirable and very ineffective in supporting our wellbeing. This is the paralyzing fear that our thoughts create by constructing imaginary, worst-case scenarios that are so powerful and convincing we react as if they were real threats when, more often than not, they are nothing but an invention of our overactive imagination.

If you stop to think about it, most of our fears never come to pass. They are 99 percent imagination and 1 percent legitimate possibility. Do bad things happen? Of course. There are no guarantees in life. But look at the things that have brought us the most fear—fear of being rejected when our opinions and behaviours don't align with others; fear of making a fool of ourselves if we attempt something new and do it badly; fear of being laughed at or humiliated; fear of being hurt if we expose our vulnerable underside; fear of reaching for something bigger than ourselves and falling flat on our face; fear of not measuring up to expectations—these non-life threatening fears, and many others, are the fears that haunt our minds and sometimes our dreams. That these fears exist at all is to be expected. Fear is the way our minds inform us that we are moving toward conditions, people, places, and events that we don't fully understand, so our mind generates fear to warn us of potential danger that may be lurking around the corner or over the horizon.

This is the condition each of us faces when we step outside our comfort zone. Fear is evidence that we are stretching beyond the familiar and entering unexplored territory. Fear is healthy. It is a powerful survival skill alerting us to unknown conditions, and it gets our attention focused on the most effective way to respond. Interpreted accurately, fear is a very beneficial aspect of our human condition. If we lacked a fear response, we wouldn't be able to determine what was safe and what was dangerous, so fear is very important in our mental tool kit.

The ineffective aspect of fear occurs when it's triggered by nothing more real than our imagination, by conditions that pose little actual danger to us but which we frequently misinterpret as a legitimate threat. This category of fear prevents us from growing into our potential. It keeps us stuck. It creates analysis paralysis. It freezes us in our present condition and suggests we're better off as we are—no matter how unsatisfactory—because at least we know our current condition. Better the devil you know than the devil you don't. The degree in which we yield to these imaginary fears is equivalent to the degree in which our life stalls, and over time we begin to feel victimized by a world around us that seems increasingly frightening and dangerous. This is how politicians justify "tough on crime" programs despite the fact that the number of violent crimes has been steadily decreasing for years. Creating a perception of danger— regardless of the actual danger—triggers fear, and people react to the perceived threat rather than to the facts.

It is this kind of fear that I want to address. Make no mistake about this. When we are in the throes of this kind of fear, it can be as powerful as the fear we experience from the mad dog on the loose. In some ways it is even more terrifying because at least we can identify the mad dog as the source of our fear. The real terror of our imaginary fears is that they can be hard to pin down. Sometimes we can identify the specifics of our fears, like the constant bombardment of violence we see on the news leading us to believe that we live in a very threatening society. But more often it is a generalized fear that triggers a flood of imaginary scenarios that wash across our mind. Lacking the capacity to make sense of them, we can become overwhelmed, which leads to knee-jerk reactions or to a state of complete paralysis.

I remember an occasion when my imaginary fears became so real that I nearly quit my job. I had recently learned to drive a tractor-trailer and was working for a company as a truck driver. For some reason I began thinking about a particular trip I had to make every week that took me through a 50-mile canyon. It was a two-lane road, and driving up the canyon put me on the outside lane that had a short cement guardrail and a cliff that dropped 100 feet into a raging river. This river is known for its powerful current. It is not a river you would ever want to fall into.

I began imagining my trailer hitting black ice, crashing through the guardrail, and careening down the cliff into the river with me attached to the trailer. I would be dragged into the water, caught in the current, and I would drown. I began thinking about my young family. As the sole breadwinner, what would they do if I died? I would never get to see them grow up. Was this job really worth it? Wouldn't I be better off if I got a job that didn't expose me to such danger? Was it worth the money to take such a risk with my own life and the future of my family? On and on these fears kept growing, and I could feel my anxiety growing with each new speculation. I started wondering how I could get a different job and wondered how much money I could make. Would it be enough to maintain our standard of living? Would it enable me to continue providing the financial resources necessary to give the kids the quality of life my wife and I desired for them?

As my mind was groping its way through these questions, I felt myself getting more and more depressed. I didn't know what to do and I couldn't think my way through to a workable solution. Becoming more and more depressed, I suddenly became aware of the heat on my leg. It broke my concentration and I looked down. I saw the book I was holding in my hand, and as I looked across the backyard I realized just how powerful my imagination was. The heat I was feeling on my leg was the sun shining on it. Outside in my backyard, in the middle of summer, I had just worked myself into a near state of panic over the possibility of hitting black ice and dying a horrible death. The absurdity of my fears hit me like a brick between the eyes. An invention of my mind, completely opposite to my current circumstances, had me seriously considering quitting my job.

This was a tremendously useful lesson for me. I realized just how powerful my imagination is and how it could transport me into a nightmare—along with the corresponding emotions of fear, panic and depression—though none of it was actually real.

Shortly after this experience, another event occurred that showed me beyond a doubt just how different and unpredictable reality can be from my imaginary fears. I was driving back to the warehouse on a flat, straight stretch of road. It was midafternoon on a clear sunny day—one of those late summer days when you can see far off into the distance and driving is effortless. As I approached an overpass, I noticed a B-train (a tractor pulling two trailers behind it) loaded with lumber sitting in the bottom of the gully that separated one side of the highway from the other. As I passed the truck on my left, I noticed the headlights of a car poking out from under the front of the truck. My heart sank.

It turned out that an old couple had pulled off to the side of the road under the overpass to fix the tarp that had blown loose on the small utility trailer full of wood they were pulling. After securing the tarp, the gentleman started the car and pulled out onto the highway. Unfortunately he didn't check to see if the road was clear. At the same moment he pulled out, the B-train—travelling 60 miles per hour, loaded with 110,000 pounds of lumber—was passing by. In the split second the truck driver had to react, he swerved to the left. He was unable to avoid collecting the couple's car and utility trailer under his front wheels, and all together they hurtled off the highway into the gully. The weight of the B-train buried the car underneath its wheels, instantly killing the couple.

As shocking and tragic as this accident was, it immediately brought to mind my imaginary fear of dying from a black ice accident in the canyon. I realized that I would never have imagined the possibility of being caught up in a fatal accident while driving along a flat, straight stretch of road in the middle of summer. Reality is unpredictable, and the scenario I was scaring myself about was as improbable as the likelihood of the accident I had just witnessed.

The timing of my imaginary fears and witnessing that accident, several weeks later, drove home to me the fact that most of the things we fear never occur, and most of the things that really test us come when we least expect them. I realized that there is no way to accurately predict when a tragedy might strike, that the nature of life is unpredictable. There is no way to anticipate every contingency, and we will drive ourselves crazy if we try to control everything in an attempt to stay safe. It occurred to me that the only way to ensure I stayed safe was to lock myself in a closet and never come out. That way nothing unexpected could happen to me. But while this solution might ensure my safety, I would need to seriously question the quality of my life.

I decided that life is life. Tragedy occurs at the intersection of unpredictable events and random chance, and it cannot be foreseen or controlled. To live fully requires us to step into the stream of life—with all its unpredictable twists and turns, its risks and rewards—into the mystery that each day presents us. We can choose to run away from life in an effort to control conditions, but life will find a way to surprise us when we least expect it. We cannot control everything, and to place that burden on ourselves is to invite ungovernable fear, anxiety, and unmanageability.

The solution to fear is to face whatever comes, to the best of our ability, trusting the God of our understanding to support us regardless of the conditions we encounter. Remember that the one power we retain is the power to choose our response to whatever life presents us with. As Victor Frankl (1963) noted, "To be sure, a human being is a finite being, and his freedom is restricted. It is not freedom from conditions, but freedom to take a stand toward the conditions." (p. 205). When we experience fear, we retain the power to respond rather than react. It is our ability to respond that increases the possibility of a positive outcome, regardless of the conditions we encounter. It is our unconditional ability to *respond* to the conditions of our life that sooths our fear and expands our peace of mind.

None of us knows if or when tragedy will strike, or when we will eventually die. What we do know is that if we are on firm spiritual ground, are living each day to the best of our ability, and striving to improve the quality of our life and the lives of everyone we touch, we create the optimum conditions to reduce our fears and increase our experience of gratitude and joy. We cannot know what the day has in store for us, but we can take comfort in the fact that, regardless of what the universe brings, we have the freedom to choose our response to whatever conditions arise.

The daily practice that reduces my imaginary fears and brings me comfort is to thank my Higher Power for each new day of life, knowing that there is a possibility it will be my last. I ask Him to guide my thoughts, perceptions, and actions to be of maximum service to Unconditional Love. Should this truly be the last day of my life, let me live it as fully and lovingly as possible so my last day on earth is a legacy of loving kindness, gratitude, and compassion. If you knew that today was your last day on earth, how would you choose to live it?

By recognizing that most of our fears are **F**alse **E**vidence **A**ppearing **R**eal, we reduce the likelihood of reacting inappropriately to imaginary terrors. Turning our will and our life over to the conscious service of Unconditional Love, we develop the courage, wisdom, and strength to

Face **E**verything **A**nd **R**ecover our capacity to fully embrace life, one day at a time, to the best of our ability.

Before leaving this topic, I would like to expand on the third kind of fear that occurs every time we step outside our comfort zone into the region of adventure, learning, and opportunity. To avoid this kind of fear is to stop growing. This kind of fear is not a sign of danger or weakness; it's a sign that our life is about to expand.

I remember one night, lying in bed feeling my heart pounding in my chest. The next day I would be facilitating a leadership workshop with a group of 24 managers and supervisors. What confused me about my pounding heart was that I had given this workshop many times before and had been training and public speaking for more than fifteen years. As I explored my fear, I couldn't find the source of it. I was very comfortable speaking in front of people, and I was completely prepared for this workshop. In short, there was no logical reason for me to be fearful. So why was my heart pounding?

As I continued to reflect on my fear, it occurred to me that while it was true—I had given this workshop many times—the next day I was giving it to a group of people I had never worked with before. While the material was familiar and I had plenty of workshop experience, this particular situation was new, and my body was informing me that I was stepping outside my comfort zone into unknown territory with this new group.

Once I realized this was the source of my pounding chest, the fear began to subside. I understood that this response was simply my body's way of informing me that I was about to do something different and that I needed to be aware of that fact. I didn't have to do anything differently. I had thoroughly prepared for the workshop, and I was confident it would be a positive experience for everyone involved. The warning my body was sending was simply its way of letting me know that there was something different about this particular experience and that I might want to take appropriate steps to ensure a positive outcome.

I realized this is what stage actors mean when they say that to be at the top of their game they need to be afraid before stepping onto the stage. It never made sense to me until this experience when I understood that having a degree of fear heightens attention and awareness, which is desirable when full attention is called for.

The next time you're experiencing a fear-based response in your body, take the time to examine the source of that fear. If you discover it's the result of stepping out of your comfort zone, applaud yourself. You are choosing to expand your experiences, and this is one of the surest ways of growing into the potential that is patiently waiting for your cooperation to blossom into the wonder you truly are.

EXPANDING SELF-AWARENESS

1. How many of my imaginary fears ever become reality?

2. Am I beginning to understand that my mind doesn't distinguish between real and imaginary fears?

3. If I knew today was the last day of my life, how would I choose to live it?

4. Am I becoming aware that comfort zone fear is a cause for celebration?

5. How can I bring more comfort zone fear into my life, knowing this is the evidence of personal growth?

APPLYING SELF-AWARENESS

On a sheet of paper, write down an imaginary fear you had that never came to pass and describe how your thinking and feelings were influenced by this fear. Then, answer the following questions.

1. What did I learn about how my thinking and feelings were influenced by this imaginary fear?

2. How might my understanding of the power of my imaginary fears change the way I deal with them in the future?

3. What emotions come up for me from this exercise?

4. Based on what I learned, what—if anything—will I change?

5. What do I hope these changes will do to improve the quality of my life?

CHAPTER TEN:

EVERYTHING WE DO MAKES
PERFECT SENSE AT THE TIME

One of the things that really hampered my growth was the self-inflicted beating I gave myself whenever I learned something new that had me judging something I did in the past. "I can't believe I was so stupid. What an idiot! What was I thinking?" Things I'd said and done in the past seemed ridiculous in light of new information or a gained perspective. These negative judgements made the process of learning about myself painful. As I became aware of this persistent pattern of reflection and self-criticism, I decided to examine this unproductive and uncomfortable learning strategy to discover a more effective and gentle approach.

I thought back to a particularly painful memory—when an elementary school teacher humiliated me in front of the class—wishing I knew then what I know now and imagining how differently that situation could have turned out. But changing that past situation is never going to happen. The simple fact is that I *didn't* know then what I know now, and no matter how badly I wish this wasn't the case, there's nothing I could have done differently at the time.

Wanting to change the results of the past based on new information is unrealistic, yet we beat ourselves up every time we learn something new, wishing we could retroactively apply it to a past situation. It is completely unfair to beat ourselves up based on knowledge we didn't have at the time for doing or thinking something in the past. Judging past actions on the basis of something we've only recently learned is unfair. I needn't feel badly because I couldn't defend myself against my elementary teacher due to the limited knowledge and skills I had at the time.

I believe that the decisions we make are the most effective choices we are capable of making based on the thoughts, perceptions, and feelings we have at that time. If we could have made a better decision at the time, we would have, but we simply didn't possess the knowledge to do otherwise. If at some later date we learn something new, then this knowledge can only be applied to our future choices, not our past.

This realization can be very helpful for us because it means we can stop beating ourselves up when we discover something new. Instead we can feel excited and grateful for the continuous expansion of knowledge that comes from acquiring new information. Curiosity and self-compassion eases our way to embracing new thoughts, perceptions, and feelings that come with new information and experiences. With practice we learn how to hold our certainties more lightly in our mind, reserving the right to change our opinions and responses as new information becomes available. With self-compassion we can safely embrace an attitude of humility (being teachable), which significantly increases the scope of what the Universe is able to offer us. Remember, the Universe never imposes Its will on us. It gives us gifts of insight and wisdom in direct proportion to our willingness to receive them.

If you are reading this book, I assume you have accumulated enough knowledge and experience to know that many of the things you were absolutely certain of at one point in your life have changed over time. With this in mind, is it not reasonable to conclude that while you may feel fairly certain about the things you believe today, there's a pretty decent chance that the Universe is going to bring some person, place, or event into your life that invites you to revise your perceptions and opinions as new information becomes available?

Through curiosity, self-compassion, and the humility to remain teachable we give ourselves an extraordinary gift. We discover that there need never come a time when we can't learn something new. There never need come a time when we become so rigid in our thinking and behaving that we lose the ability to discover another insight or perspective patiently waiting for our wits to find it.

The next time you notice your voices of judgement or criticism beating you up, or find yourself tempted to do so, because of some new insight or perspective you've encountered, I urge you to be gentle with yourself.

Remember that it is not only unkind but completely unfair to judge your past perceptions and behaviours by knowledge you didn't possess at the time. It logically follows that when you meet someone who is insisting that their truth is *the* truth, be gentle with them. Holding the thoughts they're holding, their truth does *feel* like the truth to them. Perhaps they haven't been as fortunate as you to discover that, like the rest of us, their truths are based on the sum of their thoughts and experiences up to this moment. The Universe will continue to present them with people, places, and events that invite them to learn something new that may have them releasing one truth for another. If they are as fortunate as we, they too may eventually learn to hold their truths more lightly, reserving the right to change their minds as new information becomes available. Those unwilling or unable to loosen their grip on their certainties are to be pitied, for they have stepped out of the stream of learning, and life will pass them by while they slowly fossilize.

Accepting that keeping an open mind and holding our truths lightly creates the best possible conditions for life-long learning and the expansion of our wisdom, know that we can still get stuck in old mental models and faulty assumptions. This does not indicate a fundamental flaw in our intellect; it merely represents the momentum of long-held habits. Through compassionate curiosity and unconditional acceptance, we gain the capacity to let go of out-dated and ineffective mental models, which we begin revising and replacing with more accurate and effective ones. The evidence of progress is noted by paying attention to how long it takes us to notice when we are acting on out-dated assumptions before choosing a more effective response. The critical element of growth and evolution is not whether we get stuck but how long we stay stuck before opening our hearts and minds to the Universe's infinite creative potential, which It willingly and unconditionally offers anyone who asks for it.

EXPANDING SELF-AWARENESS

1. Do I beat myself up, based on information I acquired later on, for some decision I made in the past?

2. Am I able to accept that it's unfair to judge past actions by new mental models?

3. Knowing that my perspectives change with new insights and experiences, am I willing to loosen my mental grip on my certainties?

4. Am I willing to create a positive environment through humility, compassionate curiosity, and open-mindedness to soften my judgements of past decisions?

5. Am I willing to create a positive environment through humility, compassionate curiosity, and open-mindedness to better understand the choices others have made in the past?

APPLYING SELF-AWARENESS

On a sheet of paper write: "If I was more accepting of the choices I made in the past based on what I knew at the time I would…" then complete the sentence ten times identifying how greater self-acceptance would impact your judgement of past decisions. On the backside of the same sheet of paper write: "If I was more accepting of the choices others made in the past based on what they knew at the time I would…" then complete the sentence ten times identifying how greater understanding and acceptance might impact your judgement of their past decisions. Then, answer the following questions.

1. What emotions come up for me from this exercise?

2. Based on what I learned, what—if anything—will I change?

3. What do I hope these changes will do to improve the quality of my life?

CHAPTER ELEVEN:

THE CHOICES WE MAKE

By accepting that we are responsible for our own experiences as the result of the way we choose to interpret them, it follows that we are also responsible for owning our choices about the people, events, and things we choose to bring and keep in our lives. If I am in an abusive relationship, then I need to ask myself how this relationship is benefitting me. What is it about me, not the other person, that makes my decision to stay in this unhealthy relationship a logical choice? Staying in a harmful relationship or situation is a choice we make, and the only error to be avoided is the belief that we can change this other person if only we… This is the error trap that we need to let go of. In the same way that no one can force you to feel anything you don't choose to feel, by virtue of the way you interpret their behaviour, you can't force anyone else to feel the way you want or need them to feel.

Our perceptions and feelings are the exclusive domain of our individual consciousness. No one can force us to interpret things a particular way without our cooperation. Sure, people may try to pressure us to see things their way. But if we agree with them out loud, as a way to relieve the pressure of their insistence, yet don't really believe it on the inside, then our perception, feeling, or belief hasn't changed despite what we say. What *has* changed on the inside is an awareness that we chose to keep our real thoughts and feelings hidden because we decided this was the most effective course of action at the time. It is very important that when we have these realizations we resist the temptation to beat ourselves up because we decided to say one thing while holding something else inside.

When I used to find myself in these situations, I was quick to label myself a coward and a fraud. The old tapes would start playing: "If you had any guts... If you were half a man... If you had the courage of your convictions..." On and on my self-critic would rage at me about my decision to placate the speaker and keep my real perspectives, feelings, or beliefs to myself. As you can imagine, this didn't do much for my self-esteem or my emotional wellbeing. Depression, self-loathing, disappointment, sadness, anger, resentment. These were the experiences and emotions that crowded my mind when I realized I had taken what I defined as *the easier, softer path*. In truth, these too were interpretations and not facts. They were the products of the beliefs I was holding based on how I was raised, the values of my family, community, society, etc.

Relief from this onslaught of negative thoughts and feelings occurred when I decided to reframe my internal self-judgements. The process went something like this. What if instead of beating myself up I chose a more effective internal response? What if I determined that the response I gave made sense? For example, after weighing as many variables as I could, I determined that arguing with this person wasn't going to accomplish anything. It was more convenient to simply exit the conversation by acknowledging that he had a valid perspective (based on his worldview) while holding a different perspective within myself.

Situations like these provide us with valuable information about how motivated, safe, or free we feel to express our real thoughts and feelings with a particular person or group. Our decision to acknowledge the validity of a perspective we don't necessarily agree with is our way of recognizing another person's right to perceive the world through their worldview while minimizing the risk of confrontation. This choice reveals a conscious decision to keep our perspective to our self. Rather than chastising ourselves for not expressing our perspective, we can harvest a gift of insight from compassionately examining the choice we made. We can do this by exploring how our response in this situation made sense to us. Some questions we might ask ourselves are:

- What am I telling myself about me, based on the way I chose to respond in this situation?

- Knowing that I don't feel safe or motivated to share my perspective with this person or group, do I really want to continue this relationship?

- Knowing what I know now, what—if anything—might I do differently the next time I find myself in a similar situation?

Notice that this line of inquiry focuses exclusively on us. There is no point looking outside ourselves for others to change in order for us to make different choices. As we learned earlier, each of us is absolutely and exclusively responsible for our choices and experiences.

The most effective time for this kind of compassionate inquiry is not in the heat of the moment when our mind may be overwhelmed with emotions, but later on when our mental and emotional states are calm. When we are calm, we are much more resourceful. This is the time to review the situation, our interpretation of it, how we chose to respond, etc. During this period of reflection we might recall what we were feeling and thinking at the time and how this influenced our response. Through this process of self-reflection we gain a clearer understanding of the perceptions and mental models we're holding, which enables us to consider what—if anything—we want to revise or replace based on what we learned. Every response we make is another opportunity to learn about ourselves. What we choose to do with that information is entirely up to us.

This process of observing and reflecting on our behaviours to identify the underlying perceptions, assumptions, and mental models is just that… a process. I implore you to be gentle and compassionate with yourself. Just because we now understand the role we play in our experiences doesn't mean we are suddenly relieved of every error trap we have. Our old mental models and assumptions exert a great deal of influence and it takes time for them to weaken and eventually disappear. The difference we experience from our growing understanding of the perceptions, assumptions, and mental models we operate under is that we are able to recognize their influence sooner. The moment we realize them we are free to make different choices.

Try not to burden yourself with unrealistic expectations of doing this perfectly. Like all growth and development, it occurs with baby steps, one day at a time. With practice it will become a conscious part of your daily interactions with the world. The goal is progress, not perfection. Easy does it...but do it.

Perfection is very appealing, yet I suspect if we ever achieved it in human form we would be grievously unhappy. Perfectionism is seductive because it seems to represent an ideal living condition. But it remains frustratingly remote despite our most conscientious efforts. Might the solution lie in accepting what all the great wisdom traditions have recognized? Perfection is the domain of God and not an achievable condition for we mere mortals. Perhaps there is greater wisdom in withholding perfection from sentient beings than we have supposed. In the next chapter we will explore the nature of perfection. We will see if our frustration with imperfection doesn't turn out to be one of the wisest and greatest blessings the Universe has bestowed upon us.

EXPANDING SELF-AWARENESS

1. In what ways do I attempt to force people to interpret reality the way I see it?

2. How often do I choose to keep my perspectives to myself?

3. What am I learning about those relationships where I choose to keep my perspectives to myself?

4. If I recognize that I don't feel safe or motivated to share my perspectives or feelings with others, what is keeping me in these relationships?

5. How willing am I to examine my perspectives, assumptions, and mental models based on other people's perspectives and opinions?

APPLYING SELF-AWARENESS

Take a sheet of paper and draw a line down the middle of the page. On the left hand top of the page write: "People I feel safe and/or motivated to share my perceptions and feelings with." On the right hand top of the page write: "People I *do not* feel safe and/or motivated to share my perceptions and feelings with." After identifying both groups of people, ask yourself the following questions.

1. What am I learning about the relationships I have based on the lists I created?

2. What is motivating me to continue having relationships with people I don't feel safe sharing my perceptions and feelings with?

3. What emotions come up for me from this exercise?

4. Based on what I learned, what—if anything—will I change?

5. What do I hope these changes will do to improve the quality of my life?

CHAPTER TWELVE:

THE PERFECTION OF IMPERFECTION

There is a tradition among Japanese gardeners, who, after their work is complete, scatter a handful of leaves so as to hold the inevitable turning point of the cycle of perfectionism at bay. Traditional American quilters, too, make sure there is a hidden imperfection in their handiwork.
— Carol Orsborn, *How would Confucius ask for a raise? (1995)*

One of the common frustrations we can expect to experience when we decide to develop our potential is the inevitable realization of the gap between our knowledge and our ability to apply that knowledge consistently. It's like the marriage counsellor getting a divorce. The counsellor can't help but wonder why, with all the knowledge she possesses, she can't seem to apply it to her own situation. Personally, I have spent many years trying to learn, understand, and integrate all my knowledge and experience to align my spiritual nature with my human condition, yet despite the wealth of information I have acquired, I frequently experience moments of doubt and fear about whether God is truly listening and guiding my life. If I am accurate about this dual condition of spirit and ego, and correct in assuming that the ideal strategy for securing genuine happiness and love is by placing my human consciousness (ego) in the intentional service of Unconditional Love (spiritual nature), then why do I consistently deviate from this path and find my ego once again attempting to direct my life by time-worn strategies that have repeatedly failed in the past?

Reflecting on this situation I came to realize that this condition affects virtually everyone. The most conscientious and dedicated people struggle as much as anyone else to consistently apply their knowledge and experience, and they find themselves caught up in the same alternating, ego-driven/ spiritually-directed life as everybody else. The obvious conclusion is we are lacking some essential ingredient necessary to make a permanent transition from ego-driven to spiritually-guided living. But what if this isn't the case?

It occurred to me that if our true (spiritual) nature is Unconditional Love, then our highest human potential should be realized by aligning our human consciousness with our spiritual nature. This alignment enables Unconditional Love to expand and experience Itself in form. If this assumption is accurate, we should expect to experience a steady improvement in the quality of our lives by encountering and extending Unconditional Love in our lives and the lives of everyone we touch. This has certainly been the case for me, yet it has not been a perfect case. Time after time, I lose touch with my Higher Power and my feelings of loving kindness for the world and myself. Instead I find myself feeling angry, impatient, frustrated, depressed, etc. and wonder how I came to be in this undesirable state again. What am I doing wrong? Why do these undesirable experiences continue to happen despite my confidence in the path I've chosen?

Turning this confusion over to my Higher Power (which is how I deal with things I can't figure out on my own), I relaxed and allowed my mind to drift off. Sometime later a question popped into my head. If Unconditional Love knows that my deepest desire is to align my spiritual nature with my human condition so that I can experience the genuine happiness and fulfillment I desire, then why doesn't It simply remove every obstacle that stands in the way of accomplishing this life-enhancing outcome? It isn't for lack of ability. If Unconditional Love chose to remove every limitation in my life, then I am convinced they would cease to exist the very instant Unconditional Love made the decision. If Unconditional Love has decided to leave these limitations in place, there must be a reason. Since this condition seems to be a common denominator among human beings, then it seems reasonable to suppose that these limitations must serve some important function we don't understand. So what might the benefits of these limitations be? What is the benefit of being constantly reminded that relying on the ego to direct our life increases the level of unmanageability we experience? Looked at another way, if we were able to maintain an uninterrupted relationship with Unconditional Love, what might the negative consequences be?

Viewed in this light, it occurred to me that if we were able to achieve an uninterrupted experience of unconditional love then we wouldn't need God anymore since our ego would logically conclude that we had achieved complete integration of our spiritual nature with our human condition. Having achieved this perfect union, what reason would we have to continue interacting with God? Suddenly my inability to perfectly encounter and extend unconditional love under all conditions made sense. More than that, it struck me as a brilliant insight on God's part to recognize that if our ego was ever able to conclude that this internal ego/spirit alignment was perfectly achieved, it would therefore be easy for it to conclude that it no longer needed to maintain a conscious relationship with its spiritual source; it could now assume absolute control over our life.

This conclusion is not a criticism of the ego. Rather it is an accurate assessment of just how powerful our rational, logical ego-mind is—and must be—in order for it to be able to consciously and intentionally choose to have a relationship with Unconditional Love. It is only through reflective consciousness and free will that a person can have an authentic relationship with another. The same power that enables us to enter into a voluntary relationship with the God of our understanding must be equally capable of rejecting this relationship. So what conditions would encourage our ego to enter into this relationship, which by its very nature reduces the influence of our ego in our daily life? Could it be the continuous reminder of our ego's limitations in creating the genuine happiness and fulfillment we desire?

Through a series of failed attempts, our ego gradually and grudgingly came to recognize that its strategies and "best thinking" were limited by the sum of its knowledge and experience. In choosing to align itself with the mind of God, it gained access to resources infinitely greater and more effective than its own. Since our ego sincerely desires to bring us genuine happiness and fulfillment, and has come to accept that the only way to accomplish this is by putting its resources in the service of Unconditional Love, our ego does its best to cooperate. But this is not a permanent or perfect situation from our ego's perspective.

Our ego has been consciously directing our life for a far longer period of time than it has functioned as the conscious servant of our spiritual nature. Our ego's imperative to direct our life doesn't cease to operate simply because it has come to recognize that it may not be entirely capable of producing the results it wants for us. Even when it acknowledges the benefit of subordinating its will to our spiritual nature, this subordination creates tension within the ego for supremacy of influence in our daily life. Our ego wants to be in charge, and when it recognizes that our spiritual nature is more powerful and effective in bringing us genuine happiness and fulfillment it struggles—moment to moment—to let go and let God.

The brilliance of the imperfection God imbedded within every one of us is that through the unmanageable experiences we encounter when our ego tries to run our life, we get continuous reminders of our need to consciously reach out to Unconditional Love for guidance and support. Our imperfection ensures that our ego will not be able to hijack our continued growth toward the alignment of our spiritual nature with our human condition, nor our continued desire to deepen our conscious relationship with the God of our understanding. It is in our best interest to forever strive, yet to never achieve, a perfect union with Unconditional Love while we exist in human form. The moment perfect alignment is achieved, we will no longer be human beings but pure spiritual consciousness.

Imperfection reminds us to recommit ourselves on a daily basis to the ongoing development of creating a conscious relationship with Unconditional Love through all the people, places, and events Her/He/It brings into our life to teach, guide, and support us on our journey. Imperfection ensures there will never come a time when we don't have cause to reach out to Unconditional Love and say, in whatever form, "God help me." Imperfection keeps us grounded in our relationship with Unconditional Love, Who helps us focus on those qualities of thoughts, perceptions, and feelings that increase the degree of loving kindness, compassion, empathy, and willingness we extend and encounter in our lives and the lives of everyone we touch.

This, I believe, is the wonder and elegance of God deciding to limit our capacity for perfection while in our human condition. God is wise enough to recognize that a perception of perfection would be fatal to the act of reaching out to a Power greater than ourselves. I have come to recognize and appreciate the gift of imperfection because of the crucial role it plays in motivating me to continue to reach out to Unconditional Love on a daily basis.

Sitting with these reflections, my frustration with imperfection dissolved and I was left with a sense of wonder and awe at the perfection of the mind of God to understand the paradox of imperfection as the elegant instrument by which we are continuously reminded of the necessity and benefit of reaching out in conscious cooperation with Unconditional Love.

The next time you find yourself berating yourself because you keep making mistakes, give yourself a break. Imperfection is built into the very fabric of our human condition. It reminds us to keep reaching out to each other and to the God of our understanding to improve our capacity to bring empathy, forgiveness, and loving kindness into our own lives and the lives of everyone we touch.

So ends the first stage of our journey to reclaim the life we lost along the way. Now that we have examined the richness and limitations of our current approach to life, it is now time to turn our attention to the task of recovering those lost and hidden parts of ourselves through shifting our focus from an exclusive reliance on our ego-identity to the more inclusive reliance on our unconditionally loving spiritual nature. Through this progressive shift in orientation and intention, we reintegrate all those parts of ourselves we previously judged unacceptable or as impairments to our ultimate happiness. As the coming chapters hope to reveal, by reclaiming our lost and hidden elements, we find the path that leads to securing and experiencing the quality of life we have been seeking for so long.

EXPANDING SELF AWARENESS

1. Do I feel frustrated when I find myself deviating from what I know will serve me best?

2. Do I ever find myself struggling to be compassionate, empathetic, and/ or understanding despite my best efforts to reflect Unconditional Love?

3. Am I noticing that my ego sees cooperation with my spiritual nature as a temporary condition until the chaos in my life goes away?

4. Am I beginning to see that imperfection is a gift because it inspires me to consciously reach out to Unconditional Love for guidance and support in living a happier and more fulfilling life?

5. Am I willing to give myself a break when I fail to express Unconditional Love knowing that imperfection is woven into the fabric of my ego-based human condition?

APPLYING SELF-AWARENESS

On a sheet of paper write: "If I was able to accept that imperfection is built into the fabric of my human condition I would..." then complete the sentence ten times identifying how accepting imperfection would move you from self-criticism to curiosity. On the backside of the same sheet of paper write: "If I was able to loosen my grip on striving for perfection I would..." then complete the sentence ten times identifying how surrendering the unattainable goal of perfection would open up more possibilities now that perfection is no longer required or expected. Then, answer the following questions.

1. What emotions come up for me from this exercise?

2. Based on what I learned, what—if anything—will I change?

3. What do I hope these changes will do to improve the quality of my life?

PART TWO

SELF-RECOVERY

CHAPTER THIRTEEN:

FINDING A POWER GREATER THAN OURSELVES

When my life fell apart and I became willing to let "something" other than my ego direct my life, it was suggested by people who had already started their journey of recovery that this "something" was a Power greater than myself. I had no idea how to do this, but what I did realize was that the people who were offering this suggestion reported the benefits this decision produced in their lives. If I wanted the peace, gratitude, and joy they had, then finding and surrendering my will over to this Higher Power was the way to get it. They suggested that this Power could be anything that worked for me. With nothing to lose, I made a conscious decision to try and establish some kind of connection with this Power.

I said out loud: "I may be speaking to thin air right now, but my life is a disaster, and if I'm not speaking to thin air and You can hear me and would like to have a relationship with me, then I am willing to have one with You. Since I'm not sure if You even exist, if You *do* want a relationship with me, then You are going to have to come the rest of the way, because this is as far as I can go right now."

There was no flash of light or blinding revelation following my proposal, but I slowly became aware of the compassion, empathy, and unconditional acceptance I was experiencing with this community of fellow travellers. Over time my sense of connectedness with others and a Power greater than myself began to grow, and through this growth the quality of my life began to improve.

After consciously reaching out to this unknown Higher Power, I began to notice things that had previously escaped my attention. For example,

I was absentmindedly driving to meet with this community of people when I noticed I was speeding. When I left the group later, I noticed I was driving slower than the speed limit. When I became aware of this, I discovered that it occurred after virtually every meeting. I wondered about the significance of this curious behaviour when it suddenly struck me that I was rushing to be with these people and felt reluctant to return to the lonely life I experienced when I was away from them. They filled me with a kind of loving vitality that I had never encountered before, and I couldn't get enough of it. Without fail, regardless of how I was feeling before I arrived, after connecting with them I felt more hopeful, more grateful, and more optimistic about myself and about my potential to live a more effective and abundant life. When I listened to people share their life stories of struggle and unmanageability followed by the strength, hope, and optimism they experienced as a result of finding a Power greater than themselves to guide them, I was physically moved. When I approached them later to thank them for their talk and to express how powerfully they had touched me, they would invariably ask me what it was I found so impactful. To my frustration and embarrassment, I couldn't actually remember the words they spoke but was nevertheless powerfully moved by their genuine sharing.

At first I wondered if I had suffered brain damage due to my addictive behaviour, but I realized that the impact I was experiencing was not from the stories themselves. It was from the honesty, courage, hope, and gratitude their words carried. I realized that the words they spoke were the delivery system, not the message. It was the energy of raw truth, struggle, and healing coming through their stories that was making such a powerful impression on my heart and mind.

The final piece of the puzzle that confirmed for me the existence of a loving, compassionate, and unconditionally loving Higher Power occurred when I reflected on the first time I encountered this group of people. I had just finished a bottle of wine because I was too afraid to meet them sober. When I walked through the door, people approached me, shook my hand, told me I was in the right place, and invited me to sit down and just listen. After the meeting, strangers came up to me, warmly shook my hand and genuinely encouraged me to come again because I was important and my presence really mattered to them. They told me that no matter how badly I thought about myself or how much harm I had done to others and myself, things would get better if I kept coming back.

When I left that first night, I was stunned! I couldn't believe how complete strangers could be so welcoming to someone like me, who I judged at the time to be a failure, a loser, a lost soul, bankrupt in every sense of the word. My life was broken into a thousand pieces. I felt like a piece of human garbage who would be doing the world a favour by dying so that I wouldn't cause the people I loved any more pain. I had absolutely nothing to offer these people in exchange for their kindness and friendship, yet they wanted me to come back.

Against this backdrop of self-loathing and hopelessness, these strangers not only allowed me to join their community, but they warmly encouraged me to come back. By the standards of socially appropriate behaviour, their compassionate, unconditionally accepting, and genuinely loving nature towards me defied everything I had come to know and expect from people. Upon later reflection I came to realize that this was my first exposure to a Power greater than myself. Their loving compassion and genuine concern for my welfare was the embodiment of unconditional love. It was this first encounter that provided me with tangible evidence of the existence of a Higher Power who was unconditionally loving, and this loving energy was what I experienced every time I was with these people. It was this same loving energy that was communicated through their actions and their stories that had such a powerful impact on me.

The recognition and experience of this unconditionally loving energy became the foundation of my belief that there is a force in the universe that is capable of transforming the most broken, battered, and wounded human beings into profoundly loving, compassionate, and life-affirming agents of Unconditional Love, encountering and extending Itself in our life and the lives of everyone we touch. This was not some abstract concept of God; it was Unconditional Love in action.

I have come to think of this Higher Power as Conscious Unconditional Love seeking to experience Itself in the universe. I have observed that to the extent we put our ego in the service of this Unconditionally Loving source (God, as we understand It) we achieve the alignment of our dual identities and begin to experience the beauty, wonder, and power of our true selves in relationship to ourselves and the world. I have come to believe that Unconditional Love in form is who we truly are. This is our deepest truth and purpose in life. To the extent we live this truth we discover our birthright as unconditionally loving beings sustained and supported by Unconditional Love. By living this truth to the best of our abilities, we can experience the richness and abundance that are the natural properties of Unconditional Love manifesting Itself through us.

While I have come to love and cherish the relationship I have with the God of my understanding, in my particular case this relationship developed gradually over many years before becoming deeply embedded in my thinking and living experience. I have come to observe that each of us discovers and nurtures our relationship with a Power greater than ourselves in our own unique ways. There is no "right" way to establish and grow this relationship. There are as many ways of securing this relationship as there are people in the world. Within each of us is a spark of the Infinite, and to each of us is the task and opportunity to create a working relationship with Unconditional Love—an opportunity to focus our conscious attention on developing this relationship, to the best of our ability, so that we can experience the realization of our highest potential as spiritual beings having a human experience.

As I write this I am aware of how deeply my relationship with the God of my understanding has penetrated my life, and I am grateful beyond words for the richness this relationship has provided me and all those who Unconditional Love has brought into my life to assist and support me on my journey to a more authentic, loving, and joyful existence.

Over the many years since I first came to recognize the existence of a Power greater than myself, and attempted daily to consciously align my will with this loving energy, this relationship has continued to deepen and expand. I know in the core of my being that there truly is an Unconditionally Loving Intelligence that exists and that desires to have a relationship with us to the precise degree that we want to have a relationship with It.

Let me state this in the clearest possible terms. The road to recovering our capacity to experience the fullest and most deeply satisfying dimensions of our life lies in our ability to find a Power greater than ourselves. We must do everything in our power to develop this relationship so we can begin the process of shifting control of our lives from an exclusive reliance on our ego-identity to the guiding influence of a Power greater than ourselves experienced and expressed through our spiritual identity. This is the path that leads to encountering and experiencing the genuine happiness we've been seeking.

After finding a Power greater than ourselves, the next challenge becomes deciding how to surrender more control of our ego-directed life to our spiritual identity.

- How do we find the willingness to turn our ego's conscious will over to the direction of our Higher Power?

- What conditions need to be met in order for us to voluntarily surrender control of our ego-based decision-making process to this unseen spiritual power?

The assertion that surrendering control of our ego-dominated life to our spiritual nature is the means by which we become more effective and empowered is counter-intuitive. It needs to be subjected to rigorous scrutiny before any reasonable person would be inclined or expected to act on it. It is asking too much to simply accept that the way to increase our experience of genuine happiness and fulfillment is by stepping away from the only source of empowerment we know. To take such a leap into the unfamiliar region of a spiritually directed life demands some reassurance that the decision has some foundation in logic and reason. Herein lies the task ahead. To put it plainly, is there a reasonable way to support the claim that the quality of our lives would be substantially improved by surrendering control of our daily decision-making process from a reliance on our ego-identity to our unconditionally loving spiritual nature?

SURRENDERING CONTROL

Before I became willing and able to surrender control of my life over to a Power greater than myself, I needed to satisfy two preconditions. First, that I could reasonably establish the existence of some form of self-aware consciousness independent of my conscious mind, i.e. a non-material logos that I could relate to as God. Second, that the nature of this non-material logos was unconditionally loving and had only one overarching priority: to do everything in Its power to assist and support me towards the realization of my highest human/spiritual potential.

The second precondition was a deal-breaker. If I was going to surrender the power of governing my life to some unseen force, then I had to be convinced that such a decision would genuinely improve the quality of my life. Otherwise, why bother? It also seemed self-evident that if I was going to surrender control of my life to something, I had to genuinely trust It. I needed reassurance that It was never going to set me up, or pull the rug out from under me, and that It would consistently and faithfully act in ways that moved me in the direction of becoming the most loving being I was capable of. I put these preconditions out to the Universe. The thoughts that follow reflect the outcome of this inquiry.

The first was an old saying that a tree is known by its fruit. An apple tree cannot produce a tomato because the potential for producing a tomato doesn't exist in an apple tree. Only apple trees can grow apples. For an apple to emerge, the potential for it must already be present in the tree. Applying the same logic, if self-aware consciousness is the ultimate fruit of the physical universe (as far as we know), the potential for self-aware consciousness must already be present in the universe prior to its emergence.

We know from physics that everything that exists in the universe arises from pure energy, and as energy binds together into ever more complex atomic and molecular arrangements, it becomes matter. When enough matter comes together, stars and planets are born, along with every other celestial form that exists in the universe. Through some as yet unknown process, inorganic matter became organic matter and life began. Over vast periods of time, life became more complex and gradually achieved consciousness. Over even greater periods of time, consciousness became self-aware and reflective. This is the state of human beings today.

We are self-aware consciousness by virtue of our ability to be self-reflective. We can contemplate our own existence. We can think about what we think about. Without getting into a debate as to how this process came about, the central point is to observe that everything that we think of as the universe, up to and including self-aware consciousness, arose from pure energy. In other words, self-aware consciousness is one of the 'fruits' of pure energy.

Since any fruit must exist as potential before it can exist in form, it is reasonable to conclude that the pure energy from which the universe came into existence contained within it the potential for everything that it 'grows'. Therefore, self-aware consciousness was woven into the very fabric of the universe. Since we arise out of the universe and are self-aware, by logical deduction the Universe must be self-aware. While you may argue the philosophical merits of my conclusion and choose to scrutinize this proposition more rigorously, it satisfied my first precondition by establishing a reasonable foundation for the belief that there actually is some form of self-aware consciousness, independent of my ego, interpenetrating the fabric of the universe.

The second precondition I required was to establish, with reasonable confidence, that the nature of this universal consciousness is unconditionally loving. To verify whether this was the case, I began by thinking about life forms. Can we observe life and find evidence of the unconditionally loving nature of the universe? As I began thinking about various life forms, it occurred to me that we can draw some general conclusions based on medical research. Science has conclusively demonstrated that human life requires loving encounters to support and enrich its healthy development. Human development suffers when deprived of love.

We know that a baby's physical, mental, and emotional development are enhanced when they are actively loved, held, cuddled, stroked, talked to, given eye contact, etc. We also have clinical evidence that babies who are deprived of these loving encounters experience increasingly severe physical, mental, emotional, and developmental hardships. Research on neglected orphans reported a 30% mortality rate by the age of two among children who didn't receive loving stimulation during infancy. There is also a growing body of evidence that other life forms are similarly impacted by love or its absence. It appears that life responds favourably to encounters with love and suffers when love is denied.

Recognizing the critical relationship between loving interaction and healthy development, I found it reasonable to conclude that our nature, and by logical extension the nature of the universe from which we arise, must be loving since life thrives in the presence of loving energy and suffers when deprived of it. With this evidence in hand, I felt confident in concluding that love is a foundational element of our human condition.

Since potential must exist prior to emergence, and life requires loving interaction in order to thrive, I concluded two things.

1. The universe possesses self-aware consciousness.

2. The fundamental nature of the energy that animates the universe is love.

Human beings are the physical 'fruit' of universal energy. We require loving interaction in order to develop and thrive, and we possess self-aware consciousness. Armed with these facts, I satisfied my rational mind that there was indeed a reasonable basis for concluding that there is some form of self-aware consciousness, independent of my finite human ego, whose nature is unconditionally loving.

Having satisfied these preconditions, I began to wonder: why did the Universe provide us with self-will? Why would Unconditional Love increase our struggle and make a relationship with Him/Her/It more difficult by giving us the freedom to choose or reject a relationship with It? If God is Unconditional Love and wants to experience Unconditional Love through us, what is God's purpose in giving us self-will?

It occurred to me that if God created the universe so It could experience unconditional love in physical form, then God needed to include the capacity for us to be reflectively conscious and possess free will. I support this conclusion based on my belief that genuinely loving relationships require free will to be authentic. By authentic I mean we are free to enter into a conscious relationship with another and equally free to reject that relationship, if we so choose. Only through freedom of choice is a truly authentic loving relationship possible. This, I believe, explains how it is possible for us to reject our spiritual nature and attempt to govern our lives by our ego-based identity, as though our existence was somehow independent of the Universe out of which we arose.

Earlier I suggested that to the degree we depart from our identity as spiritual beings having a human experience, we deny our most fundamental nature. This denial represents an attempt to psychically sever our existence from the source, acting as though it is separate and independent of everyone and everything else in the universe. In essence our claim of being separate and independent is to claim the position of God in our own lives. If this is an error trap, then the nature of this error must ultimately reveal itself through increasing levels of unmanageability and suffering.

Having chosen to be the God of our own life, many of us have discovered how lonely and confusing this choice is. Having to figure everything out and relying exclusively on our own 'best thinking' to solve the challenges and struggles we face can become overwhelming. Eventually we discover that it simply isn't possible to exert enough control over others and the larger world to ensure the results we want. As this realization takes root, we can't help but wonder if there might not be a more effective approach to securing the quality of life we desire.

As our struggles and dissatisfaction expand, the pressure to solve things on our own becomes increasingly great. We find ourselves beginning to question whether we've missed some important insight or essential element, without which we can never achieve the life we so desperately want. This is another "hitting bottom" moment. This is the moment when we are sick and tired of being sick and tired of maintaining our claim to being the God of our own existence and the source of our own solution. This is the moment we decide to open the door of willingness a crack—willingness to consider a different approach to governing our lives.

Willingness to challenge our assumptions and mental models about self-sufficiency and self-reliance is all that's required to begin the process of realigning the relationship between our ego-based identity and our spiritual nature. Through this realignment we begin to achieve the healthy integration of our spiritual nature with our human condition. As this integration continues, we are naturally (ontologically) drawn into a deeper exploration and conscious relationship with a Power greater than ourselves. Through this conscious relationship we discover that the quality of our thinking changes; as our thinking changes, so too does our behaviour. And as our behaviour changes, our experience of life begins to change as well.

The life we were living, cut off from the source of our existence, is gradually replaced through a deepening relationship with the God of our understanding. As this relationship grows, it reflects and expands our true nature, which is a self-aware conscious expression of Unconditional Love in form. Our entire perspective of self, others, and the Universe begins to change.

If an unconditionally loving God really exists, and if this God truly desires to engage in an authentic relationship with us—contingent only on our desire to have a relationship with Him/Her/It—then by choosing this relationship we should expect to see the quality of our lives improve. The evidence of our improving quality of life ought to include increasing levels of manageability, gratitude, and joy. This is precisely what occurred for me as I began this journey from isolation to reunion with my own deepest nature as an unconditionally loving spiritual being having an imperfect human experience with the God of my understanding.

One concrete example of how the quality of my life improved was my ability to overcome my fear of spinning an airplane. To complete my pilot training I had to master the aerobatic manoeuver of putting my plane into a spin and then restoring it to straight and level flight. The manoeuver is not particularly complicated, but requires a clear and calm head to perform a specific series of steps to recover from the spin. I knew that I had to master this manoeuver in order to get my pilot's license and to feel absolutely confident when flying with passengers, so I decided to fly to the training area and practice the manoeuver until I mastered it. I had some fear about preforming the manoeuvre without a flight instructor on board. I knew that fear was the resistance to be overcome, so I had a conversation with my Higher Power about it.

The conversation sounded something like this: "Higher Power, You have provided me with this amazing opportunity to learn how to fly an airplane, something I never dreamed would be possible. To complete this goal, I need to master the spin manoeuver. I know how to technically accomplish this, and I know that the only thing that will screw me up is if I panic. I believe with all my heart that you helped me to get sober and find a relationship with You so that I could discover and realize my potential. I believe that becoming a safe and competent pilot is one of the gifts you have given me. To realize this gift, I need Your help. I need to know that I can count on You to be with me even when I am in a potentially life threatening situation. I need to know that You are a real force in my life and that You will provide me with the calm and clear state of mind I need to successfully execute this manoeuver."

With that done, I flew up to 6000 feet and performed four spin and recovery manoeuvres. Each time I performed the manoeuvre I was completely calm, my flight controls precise, and I didn't experience even a hint of fear. With each success my state of euphoria and confidence grew. After completing the four manoeuvres I knew two things with absolute certainty.

(1) I had mastered the spin manoeuvre and knew that should this situation ever occur, I had the skill to successfully recover from it.

(2) That my Higher Power was not some abstract concept limited to Sunday morning services but a living force in my life Whom I could count on to support me regardless of the situation I found myself in. As the result of this experience, I realized the concrete benefits of trusting my Higher Power to be a practical force in my life.

It was after this experiment that I made the conscious decision to turn my will and my life over to the care of the God of my understanding. I asked my Higher Power to help me deepen my spiritual relationship with Him and to help me put my heart and mind in the conscious service of Unconditional love, to the best of my ability, one day at a time.

Since I made the conscious decision to be of service to Unconditional Love, the quality of my life, and the lives of those I interact with, has immeasurably improved. I continue to strive, on a daily basis, to deepen my relationship with my Higher Power, trusting Unconditional Love to support me on my journey towards the realization of my highest human potential through the conscious alignment of my ego with my spiritual nature. This alignment has not only enabled me to overcome countless fears that might have prevented me from growing, it has brought me a richness of life and relationships I could not have imagined possible when I was running my life exclusively from my ego-based identity.

To begin the daily process of surrendering control of our decisions to a Power greater than ourselves, we can start by getting into the habit of checking in with our Higher Power first thing in the morning and asking for His guidance and support before we step into the day. My particular approach is very simple. It sounds something like this: "Thank you, Higher Power, for another day of life. I offer You my heart, my mind, my body, and my being into the service of Unconditional Love. Thank you for all the abundance you bring into my life, and thank you for providing me with all the resources I need to encounter and extend Unconditional Love into my life and the lives of everyone I touch today." That's it!

What I've noticed is that every time I take these few minutes in the morning to consciously align my ego-based identity with my spiritual nature, the quality of my day is invariably more satisfying and the challenges are more easily and effectively managed. When I forget to invite my Higher Power to direct my day, then the quality of that day is less satisfying and the challenges more difficult to manage. This relationship is consistent. When we consciously put our ego-identity in the service of our spiritual nature, our quality of life improves. When we don't make this conscious alignment, the quality of our day and our interactions with self and others suffers. What's true is what works.

However you understand God—as a Higher Power, the Universe, Unconditional Love, Great Spirit, etc.—is a matter of personal choice. There is no right or wrong about this because none of us, limited by our finite ego consciousness, can possibly embrace the magnitude of the force that we think of as God. Whatever God is, we can be sure that it is a power greater than our human mind's capacity to wholly comprehend. For this reason, our attempts to describe and define God are limited approximations and fall far short of that Conscious Unconditionally Loving Power we refer to as God.

If we can agree that our concept of God, however we conceive of It, is limited by reason of our finite imagination, then all we really need to know is that the nature of our Higher Power—however we define Her/Him/It—is Unconditional Love and that we arise from It. If this is accurate then the relationship we are seeking with the God of our understanding is already within us, waiting patiently for us to choose to have a conscious relationship with It. To put it another way, Unconditional Love is seeking to have a conscious encounter with Itself through us, and to do that it needs our independent self-aware conscious cooperation to invite It into a relationship with us. It is this conscious choice to have a relationship with Unconditional Love that enables It to extend and experience Itself in the world through our loving intentions and actions.

This relationship with a Power greater than ourselves doesn't seek to replace our rational conscious mind with blind faith but to enhance it through conscious union with our spiritual nature. Since Unconditional Love is just that—unconditional—it will never violate our right to reject that relationship and go it alone. Only when we seek It will It appear, and any time we want to take back control of our life and start running the show alone, Unconditional Love will simply step aside and wait for us to make another choice. Unconditional Love will never interfere with our free will because it is only our free will that makes an authentic relationship with Unconditional Love possible.

I started out conceiving of God as the embodiment of those qualities and characteristics I saw in people I admired and respected. Then I came to think of God as the loving force behind the universe. Eventually I came to think of God as an intelligently conscious, unconditionally loving force that extends that force into the physical universe to experience Itself in form. I have no idea how my thinking of God will continue to change, and I'm not really concerned about it. All I need to know today is that the God of my understanding is aware of me, desires a conscious unconditionally loving relationship with me, and I can trust It completely to positively shape and influence my life.

I have found a relationship with the God of my understanding that works for me today, and I implore you to do the same. Don't worry if your concept doesn't agree with anyone else's. If I have learned one thing on this journey it is that each of us has a unique relationship with life and a unique relationship with Unconditional Love.

With regard to determining whether a belief in a Power greater than you is an error trap, I encourage you to use the same standard of evaluation as with every other error trap. Test it out and observe how the quality of your experience changes as you seek to deepen your relationship with the God of your understanding. If it is an error trap, the quality of your life will worsen. If it is accurate, the quality of your life will improve. Don't take my word for it. Test it out for yourself. The proof is in the results.

I can assure you that all that's required to begin surrendering your ego-based decision-making process to your spiritual nature is the willingness to explore a conscious relationship with your Higher Power. Everything you require to deepen that relationship will appear through the people, events, and things your Higher Power brings into your life to assist you on your journey in recovering your true nature. As this relationship develops and deepens, you will begin to experience the benefit of turning your will and life over to the direction and care of this unconditionally loving Power. As we continue to surrender our ego-based identity to our spiritual nature, our sense of gratitude and genuine happiness expands. Our fears diminish as we begin to encounter the joy of life that we secretly hoped was possible but had become increasingly doubtful of ever experiencing.

As our thinking shifts from directing our lives by the limited power of our ego-based identities to becoming conscious servants of Unconditional Love, people, events, and things that genuinely improve the quality of our experience show up in our lives. The positive changes we experience encourage us to deepen our commitment to our relationship with the God of our understanding, and through this voluntary cooperation, a new freedom and joy of living begins to emerge.

Despite the benefits that are readily observable when we choose to surrender control of our life from our ego-based identity to our Unconditionally Loving spiritual nature, the challenges of moving beyond our ego-based identity are various and powerful. It is essential that we examine how this process is perceived and experienced by our ego, for it is only with the cooperation of our ego that this transformation is possible. This is the exploration we will undertake next.

EXPANDING SELF-AWARENESS

1. Am I aware that Unconditional Love is seeking a voluntary, conscious relationship with me to help me improve the quality of my life and the lives of everyone I touch?

2. Am I willing to give myself permission to establish a conscious relationship with the God of my understanding?

3. What will I do to continue deepening and expanding my relationship with a power greater than myself?

4. What are the practical benefits of trusting Unconditional Love to guide and support me as I journey through my life?

5. Am I becoming convinced that my ego-dominated approach to living is insufficient to create the quality of life I want?

APPLYING SELF-AWARENESS

Take a sheet of paper and draw a line down the middle of the page. On the left hand top of the page write: "Managing my life by self-will." On the right hand top of the page write: "Inviting Unconditional Love to guide my life." Identify as many thoughts and feelings as you can that arise when managing your life from these two stances, then ask yourself the following questions.

1. What do I gain from managing my life by self-will?

2. What is the downside of managing my life by self-will?

3. What do I gain from inviting Unconditional Love to manage my life?

4. What is the downside of inviting Unconditional Love to manage my life?

5. What emotions come up for me from this exercise?

6. Based on what I learned, what—if anything—will I change?

7. What do I hope these changes will do to improve the quality of my life?

CHAPTER FOURTEEN:

MOVING BEYOND OUR EGO-BASED IDENTITY

One of the hurdles we must overcome when seeking to live from our spiritual identity is the resistance of our ego as it fights to retain control over our life. Our ego constructs our identity based on its interpretation of the people, events, and things we've encountered in our life. It operates on the assumption that its interpretations are accurate and believes that it understands how to get us the love and happiness we yearn for.

Over the course of our life, our ego-based identity evolves. If we experience too much suffering, our ego changes certain aspects of our perceptions, beliefs, and behaviours in the hope that doing so will bring us greater happiness. Maybe we change political parties, religious practices, jobs, friends, spouses, etc. Each attempt has one ultimate goal: to increase our happiness and reduce our suffering.

Despite our ego's best efforts, many of us eventually reach the conclusion that the life we are living—while seemingly reasonable and logical—is not bringing us the genuine happiness and fulfillment we hoped for, and we begin to lose confidence in our ego-dominated approach to life. If genuine happiness cannot be secured by our ego, perhaps the answer lies elsewhere.

Looking for alternative approaches arouses tension and fear for our ego-based identity as we begin to question the assumptions and mental models our ego has been operating under. After scrutinizing the way we've been living, we discover we have no idea how to live any other way. All we have is a vague sense that perhaps we're missing something. Perhaps there is a deeper truth about who we are and how we might live more effectively that is struggling to reveal itself.

This period of discontent and confusion is the time when we are called upon to have the willingness, courage, and patience to stay in this no-man's-land a while and trust that a deeper truth will reveal itself. Having been raised in a world that celebrates instant gratification and the immediate relief from suffering, the idea of resting in our discomfort, our 'not knowing', seems alien and unreasonable. Indeed, by all the standards we've been taught, is to be avoided at all costs. As William J. Gordon observed:

> *All problems present themselves to the mind as threats of failure. For someone striving to win in terms of a successful solution, this threat evokes a mass response in which the most immediate superficial solution is clutched frantically as a balm to anxiety… Yet if we are to perceive all the implications and possibilities of the new, we must risk at least temporary ambiguity and disorder.*

The good news is that the discomfort and confusion accompanying this stage of our recovery is evidence that signals our progress. Our discomfort comes from the growing realization that we are more than our ego-dominated perceptions, beliefs, feelings, and behaviours. We are more than who we think we are. Our doubts about the way we've been living so far, and the conclusion that something's missing in our approach to life, signals the start of releasing our exclusive reliance on our ego-dominated identity. This letting go is a critical step towards recovering our spiritual identity. As we begin to consciously include the perspective of unconditional love in our decision-making process—i.e. "What would unconditional love do in this situation?"—we are able to perceive the method for achieving the successful integration of our ego-based identity with our spiritual nature.

As you can imagine, our willingness to go through this period of confusion and discomfort is only possible once we've hit bottom and come to the conclusion that our current approach to living is no longer an option.

Everyone who chooses to move beyond the limitations of their ego-based identity by integrating their spiritual nature goes through this process. It is not for the timid, but it is within the capacity of every human being whether we realize it or not. Many will choose to stay in their ego-based identity because as ineffective as it may be, at least it's a familiar discomfort. But for those of us who cannot and will not tolerate going through the rest of our lives half-fulfilled, this journey—while sometimes confusing and uncomfortable—signals the birth pains of a richer and more authentically fulfilling life brought about by consciously aligning our ego-based identity with our unconditionally loving spiritual nature.

How is this conscious alignment between our ego-identity and our spiritual nature ultimately accomplished? It begins by understanding that we have two distinct aspects to our reality as human beings. One aspect is our human condition; the other is our spiritual nature. Our human condition is temporary, existing within the realm of form, space, and time. It is impermanent and will end when we die. It is our body and our conscious mind, and when the body dies, our conscious mind departs our body. The other aspect of our reality is our spiritual nature. It exists outside the realm of form, space, and time. It is infinite and eternal. It is the energy that makes our existence possible. All matter and life in the universe arises from this spiritual energy, a conscious and unconditionally loving energy that has one goal...to express and experience Itself in physical form.

Our yearning for authentic love arises from our spiritual nature seeking to experience and express itself through our human condition. Since our ego is a function of our human condition, it cannot bring us the love and genuine happiness we're seeking independent of our spiritual nature. This explains why the more we consciously encounter and extend our unconditionally loving spiritual nature in our life and the lives of everyone we interact with, the more unconditional love we experience and the happier we become. The love we seek is within us and it needs our conscious cooperation to expand and flourish.

Our ego-identity is a conscious toolkit composed of the sum of our thoughts, assumptions, mental models, feelings, memories, behaviours, and experiences. It cannot create, manipulate, or control the spiritual source from which it arises. It cannot steal unconditional love (our spiritual nature) from the source of unconditional love (the God of our understanding) and then claim to be the creator of that love. As Ken Wilber (1998) accurately observed, "One's own ego cannot impose on the universe a view of reality that finds no support from the universe itself." (p. 32)

When operating independently of our spiritual nature, our ego draws on the data it gets from our five senses then applies logic, reason, and association to interpret reality. The ego's ultimate goal is to provide us with the love we desire, and while it hasn't yet been able to deliver on this promise, it believes it will if we give it enough time to figure the "problem" out. However, our ego's inaccurate interpretation of reality and the ego-based identity that logically follows from these interpretations is the "problem" we need to overcome. The "problem" can only be resolved when we transition from an exclusive reliance on our ego-based identity to a conscious, cooperative relationship with our spiritual nature.

As we begin this transition, our ego experiences fear as its influence over our decision-making process weakens. It fears being replaced and ultimately destroyed. To our ego, this transition feels like a death sentence. Perceived through its own frame of reference, it is a kind of death—but not the actual death it imagines. What our ego fails to consider is that there is a very good reason why we have an ego, and our journey forward is impossible without its active participation and continuous involvement. Our ego is not just an afterthought from the spiritual realm; it plays an essential role in facilitating and supporting our spiritual nature. It is through our ego consciousness that Unconditional Love can encounter and express itself in the physical universe.

Beyond the fear of losing control, our ego may experience other forms of resistance. This resistance might sound something like:

- If I let go of my ego and surrender my decision-making process over to my spiritual nature, I'm afraid I will lose not only those parts that hurt me but also those parts that bring me joy.

- If I surrender my ego, what will be left of me?

- How can I experience happiness if I reject everything I think of as me?

- I don't want to turn into some kind of mindless unconditionally loving zombie, incapable of experiencing the full range of my conscious human life, even if it means I never reach my potential.

As it turns out, these fears are groundless. When we put our conscious identity in the service of our spiritual nature, not only do we not lose our capacity to experience the full range of our human condition, we actually create the conditions for a degree of authentic joy and genuine happiness that our ego is incapable of creating or providing us on its own. Let me illustrate how this transition works by drawing on an experience many of us are familiar with.

When I was a child, Halloween held a special place of excitement and importance in my life. For days, my brother and I would plan our route to try and figure out how we could reach the maximum number of houses in the shortest period of time to get as much candy as possible. This planning brought us as much joy and excitement as the actual trick-or-treating. Day by day, our anticipation grew and we were nearly out of our minds with excitement when the day finally arrived.

If someone had told us that one day we would no longer celebrate Halloween, we would have recoiled in horror from the very idea. As a child it was inconceivable to imagine that such a thing would or could be possible and if—by some horrible set of circumstances—it did occur, it would be a tragic loss over which we would surely never recover. The loss of one of the central joys in our childhood, and the sense of fear and sadness created by the prospect that it might be taken away, can hardly be overstated.

Yet with the passing years, from children to young adults, Halloween did indeed lose its central place in our reckoning of special and exciting events. Over time, it was painlessly eclipsed by other events and activities that grew more important. What to us as children seemed like an unimaginable horror, turned out to be no tragedy at all. In fact, Halloween transitioned into fond memory so effortlessly it now takes a conscious effort to remember the central importance it played in our young lives.

The excitement with which we clung to Halloween as children, and the horror we feared were we to lose it, is precisely the desperate fear our ego is experiencing as it contemplates the horror of considering the loss of its central role in our life. It too cannot see past the conditions of the moment, and within its limited perspective, it cannot even imagine so horrible a thought as the loss of itself in the driver's seat of our life. But this fear, while completely understandable from the ego's limited perspective, is like Halloween. It is the fear of a child unaware of the many greater wonders that will effortlessly eclipse this reality. If we choose to step beyond our childlike, ego-dominated worldview to embrace the full conscious maturity that arises when we align and integrate our ego-identity with our spiritual nature, we can begin to live as fully integrated beings.

As this integration unfolds, we continue to have complete access to our past. Just because Halloween no longer excites us, doesn't mean we can't fondly remember the excitement it brought us as children. That memory always makes me smile and, for the length of my reflection, takes me back to the pure pleasure and innocent excitement that Halloween brought my brother and me as children. In the same way, the transition from exclusive reliance on our ego to a maturing reliance on our spiritual nature brings with it everything we were before. We don't lose our consciousness or our memories or our joys and sorrows. We still have complete access to our ego-identity, and at any instant we can revisit any part that strikes our fancy.

This transition isn't an *either/or;* it's a *both/and* process. We don't lose what we were, we gain what we lost access to so many years ago. Integration enables us to experience the rich, dynamic reality of who we truly are. The fundamental difference between our exclusive reliance on our ego and our conscious decision to realign it with our spiritual nature is the expanded quality of life, joy, and genuine happiness that comes with this maturing process.

Our ego is our mental child clinging to the familiar experience of being in control. It is incapable of understanding or imagining any world beyond its present condition, so any suggestion of letting go of control is terrifying to it. But as adults we have a broader perspective, and while we can assure the child that there are greater wonders than Halloween to experience, this proclamation falls on deaf ears. The reasoning of a child is perfectly logical. It is not 'wrong' per se, merely immature because it lacks the fuller and more accurate perspective of an adult.

It is by recognizing that our growth towards full maturity and the life we were born to live is dependent on our ability to let go of childhood perceptions that we are able to make this transition. We do not abandon our ego in our forward march towards recovering our true self; rather, our ego-identity becomes an active participant in supporting our journey. Our ego will always play a central role. It would make no more sense to eliminate our ego than it would to eliminate our childhood.

This is the wonder and beauty of our growth from exclusive reliance on our ego to a cooperative partnership with our spiritual nature. We bring all of our past with us. Our integrated identity is enriched by the inclusion of each memory and experience we've ever had. It is precisely this fact that enables us to rationally compare the quality of life we experience during periods of ego-reliance with the quality of life we experience during periods of spiritual alignment. This comparison enables us to determine which orientation is truly capable of improving the quality of our life.

The experience of countless individuals who have conducted this comparison reveals that the relative joy and benefits of exclusive reliance on our ego-identity is effortlessly eclipsed by the beauty, wonder, and power we experience when we choose to live in alignment with our spiritual nature.

The proper role of our ego is not to be the director but the servant of our unconditionally loving spiritual nature. Putting our ego in the service of our spiritual nature involves consciously acknowledging that Unconditional Love is a better director of our life than our ego is. Orienting our life from the perspective of: "How can I consciously serve Unconditional Love today?" dramatically improves the quality of our life and makes possible the realization of our highest potential. Our ego functions as the conscious medium that enables Unconditional Love to experience Itself through the lens of our human condition.

Rather than the death our ego fears, what it discovers is that this realignment brings a huge relief. It frees the ego from having to be the centre of the universe. The ego no longer has to play God. It no longer has to have all the answers, figure everything out, find ways to reconcile the past, predict the future, and deal with all the guilt, remorse, blame, fear, anxiety, expectation, and uncertainty it used to deal with. Relieved of all these demands, the ego is able to relax into its proper function—to become conscious of the present moment, to place its considerable strengths and capabilities under the guiding influence of its unconditionally loving spiritual nature and direct its liberated attention to the beauty, wonder, and power of Unconditional Love in all its extraordinary variety, moods, colours and textures, its mystery and its revelations.

When our ego is no longer preoccupied with having to run our life, it is freed up to pay attention to the world around it—the beauty of a tree or a flower or a cloud or the sound of children playing. It is free to focus fully on the conversation with another, rather than being preoccupied with saying or doing the "right" thing to gain approval or recognition or some other specific result it thinks necessary for our happiness. When our ego is serving our spiritual nature, it begins to notice Unconditional Love all around it in the people, places, events, and things it encounters.

Our ability to be present to the unfolding universe suddenly begins to expand. Rather than being distracted by yesterday's regrets and tomorrow's expectations, our ego can rest easy in the perfect embrace of Unconditional Love. Our life becomes richer and happier. From this realignment, the ego finds itself a willing and active participant in experiencing and expressing Unconditional Love, and we begin to encounter the genuine happiness and fulfillment our ego was unable to provide while attempting to run our life on its own.

Knowing all this and even agreeing with it is not enough to bring it about. To accomplish the transition we need to practise putting our ego in the service of our spiritual nature on a continuous basis. With so much at stake, it behoves us to examine some practical methods to establish and strengthen this life-enhancing practice.

MAKING A DAILY DECISION

Like any healthy relationship, the relationship we have with our Higher Power is not achieved and sustained by a single decision. It requires a series of decisions that we consciously choose on a daily basis. Even the most spiritually integrated human beings move between self-will (ego) and God's will (spirit) countless times every day. Securing and strengthening our relationship with our spiritual nature is a dynamic dance between our ego and our spirit. Our daily challenge and opportunity is to learn how to nurture this dynamic relationship so our decision-making process is influenced more by our unconditionally loving nature than our ego-based identity.

As noted in the chapter on surrendering control, each of us is unconditionally free to accept or reject a conscious relationship with the God of our understanding. We are free to decide how much of a relationship we want to have with our Higher Power. Unconditional Love never judges or punishes us for the choice we make. It doesn't hold a grudge. It doesn't get resentful. Unconditional Love is unconditionally loving, accepting, compassionate, understanding, wise, empathetic, welcoming, and patient because that is Its perfect nature. What It does is accurately reflect our choices through the natural and logical consequences that flow from them. When our choices are ego-based, our focus is on the outcome and our experience is a reflection of how successful we were in achieving our goal. When our choices are guided by our spiritual nature, our focus is on output and our experience is a reflection of how much unconditional love we were able to express regardless of outcome. The moment we invite Unconditional Love into our life, our orientation shifts from outcome to output and our experience changes. We are free to change our orientation as many times as we want, confident in the knowledge that every time we knock on the door of Unconditional Love, It will lovingly open.

Despite a host of concrete examples of my Higher Power's positive influence in my life, I regularly take back my will and try to run things exclusively from my ego-based identity. The obvious question is why? Why would we take our self-will back when doing so reduces our experience of genuine happiness?

My best guess is that due to the unlimited freedom to accept or reject a relationship with our Higher Power—and the momentum of habit created by having lived from our ego-based identity for so long—our attention shifts from spirit, to ego, to spirit, to ego many times each day. I used to find this very frustrating but have come to discover that this is not a cause for concern.

Having determined that the quality of our life truly is more effective and abundant when we engage in a conscious, voluntary relationship with Unconditional Love, our task is to notice when our ego is trying to run our life again and then invite our Higher Power back into the driver's seat to guide our thoughts, feelings, beliefs, and actions. The measure of our progress is how long we stay in self-will before noticing and turning our self-will back over to the guiding influence of our Higher Power. The more we practice turning our will over to our Higher Power, the easier it becomes, and the more our daily experience improves.

Our journey is not about achieving perfection; it's about making progress. I take my will back every day and I have no reason to believe this is ever going to change. The goal of our journey is not the perfect application of unconditional love in all circumstances. If we were able to achieve this, we would be perfect Unconditional Love (i.e. God), which we're not. We are imperfect human beings.

To experience unconditional love is the longing of every human being, and this longing is Unconditional Love's way of encouraging us to continue experimenting with our choices and strategies until we once again remember that the love we seek is inside us waiting patiently to be invited back into our life.

Our ongoing journey is to keep moving in the direction of reuniting our human condition with our unconditionally loving nature. It is through this alignment that our true self, in relationship with our Higher Power, is recovered. It is when we put our ego-identity in the conscious service of our spiritual nature that the quality of our living experience shifts from control to surrender, outcome to output. From unmanageability to manageability, from fear to love, from struggle to serenity. The reunion with our true self is the foundation upon which we can build the life we were born to live. As we get more and more in touch with our unconditionally loving nature and the source from which it arises, our whole orientation towards ourselves and everyone we touch begins to change for the better.

Unconditional Love seeks only to multiply Itself, and as we consciously experience our own loving nature, we discover that at the core of every other living being is the same unconditionally loving nature. With the recovery of our true self, our way of interacting with the world begins to change in the most profoundly loving and abundant ways. The fruit of living from our true self is a life of increasing joy, gratitude, compassion, self-worth, and genuine happiness.

The prospect of securing greater happiness in our life dominates our thinking, feelings, beliefs, and behaviours. The world, through various forms of media and social and cultural conditioning, suggests that happiness is contingent on things outside of us being a certain way. If we only have this job, this house in this neighbourhood, this trophy husband or wife, this car, these clothes, this kind of liquor…then we will be happy. The problem, of course, is that there are people who have all these things, yet they are deeply unhappy. So where is this illusive happiness that the world has promised us?

The answer turns out to be by securing the opposite of what the world suggests. Genuine happiness cannot be found in conquest and accumulation. Rather, it is found by developing a conscious relationship with the God of our understanding and then encountering and extending unconditional love in our interactions with everyone and everything we encounter along our journey. Turning away from the logical but inaccurate suggestions of the world is the final step on our journey of self-recovery.

As we gain a more accurate understanding of the source and nature of genuine happiness and fulfillment, the influence of the world begins to recede and our relationship with it begins to shift from a focus on getting as many things and experiences as possible before we die to the profoundly more satisfying and rewarding orientation of seeking deeper and more expansive encounters with Unconditional Love through more authentic encounter with ourselves and everyone we interact with.

It is time to address the question that has captivated our imagination and propelled us across all the years and countless decisions we have made in our life. By what means can we fully achieve the genuine happiness we are yearning for?

EXPANDING SELF-AWARENESS

1. Does it ring true that any healthy relationship requires a series of conscious decisions rather that a single formal decision?

2. Does it make sense that perfect Unconditional Love (God) must be infinitely patient and accessible because these are characteristics of Unconditional Love's very nature?

3. Does it seem reasonable that my progress, in turning my will over to the God of my understanding, ought to be evaluated by how long I stay in self-will rather than some impossible standard of perfect alignment with God since human beings are, by definition, imperfect?

4. Am I willing to view my relationship with Unconditional Love by the standard of progress not perfection?

5. As I start my practice of turning my will and my life over to the guidance and support of my Higher Power, am I willing to discover that the love I've been seeking was inside me all along waiting patiently for my free will to invite it into my daily life?

APPLYING SELF-AWARENESS

On a sheet of paper, make a list of times when you have experienced any form of Unconditional Love, then answer the following questions.

1. What form did Unconditional Love manifest in?

2. As I start noticing these myriad forms of Unconditional Love, does my awareness of them begin to expand?

3. Is the frequency of moments where I am conscious of Unconditional Love increasing?

4. What is the meaning I make from this realization?

5. What emotions come up for me from this exercise?

6. Based on what I learned, what—if anything—will I change?

7. What do I hope these changes will do to improve the quality of my life?

CHAPTER FIFTEEN

GENUINE HAPPINESS IS AN INSIDE JOB

The fountain of contentment must spring up in the mind, and he who hath so little knowledge of human nature as to seek happiness by changing anything but his own disposition, will waste his life in fruitless efforts and multiply the grief he proposes to remove.
— *Samuel Johnson*

In previous chapters I have touched on some of the qualities and characteristics of genuine happiness and how we might experience more of it in our lives. Because genuine happiness holds such a profound place in the estimation of our quality of life, I want to give it the attention and focus it deserves by understanding as clearly as possible what it is and how we can more effectively experience and express it in our lives and the lives of everyone we touch.

To begin, I want to distinguish between pleasure and genuine happiness. Short-term conviviality, levity, and the positive feelings one might experience when dancing at a nightclub, watching a comedy, or buying a new car are characteristics of pleasure. The experience of an intimate conversation, witnessing your child achieve a significant milestone in their life, or receiving the gratitude of a dear friend who you helped overcome a tragedy are characteristics of genuine happiness. The distinction lies in the degree and quality of the emotional experience. For the purposes of this investigation, pleasure is characterized as a superficial and temporary experience, whereas genuine happiness is characterized by more profound and life-altering experiences. The promises we hear in commercials suggest genuine happiness is a quick fix found in the purchase of a product or service, but what they really offer us is short-term pleasure. By contrast, genuine happiness is a deeper and more life-affirming experience brought about by an intimate connection with others and the universe.

For much of our lives we have been encouraged—through movies, books, TV shows, and commercial messaging among other things—to believe that genuine happiness is the result of something occurring outside of us. This constant stream of messaging suggests that the way to secure the genuine happiness we desire is to acquire that external "something." It might be a new car, a house, a new outfit, a facelift, more money, fame, power, romance, etc., but in each and every case the message suggests a direct relationship between acquiring something external and experiencing the genuine happiness we desire.

The difficulty in identifying the error trap in these messages is that there is a grain of truth to them. All of us have experienced the short-term pleasure that occurs when we get something new. And in the short-term, we generally would describe ourselves as being happier as a result of this external item or event. The nature of the error trap is revealed when we recognize the temporary, superficial nature of the pleasure those external conditions provide us.

Because pleasure from external elements is short lived, we soon find ourselves looking to acquire the next new "something" because the novelty of our last "something" has faded away and with it our experience of pleasure. Based on the faulty logic of this error trap, we find ourselves acquiring the next "something" in the hopes that it will fulfill the promise of bringing us genuine happiness. This is the logic behind consumer marketing, which exists to encourage continuous consumption in order to reacquire the genuine happiness that the last "something" failed to sustain.

One of the reasons we are so attracted to novelty is the escalating level of euphoria we experience as we get closer to acquiring the object of our desire. Scientific research shows that the neurochemicals that stimulate our experience of euphoria reach their peak just before we secure the object of our desire. Once the object of our desire is secured, these neurochemicals stop being produced and our euphoria immediately begins to fade. This is how our euphoria is replaced with the stress of dealing with the complications of the object we just acquired. The transition from euphoria to stress is known in the business world as buyer's remorse. It is a common experience that follows the purchase of something. While the thought of purchasing something novel is euphoric, the experience that follows is frequently one of stress and regret. Start paying attention to commercials and you will notice that they focus exclusively on the euphoria of how wonderful life will be if you purchase their product. They never mention the stress and complications that arise once the purchase is made.

I am not suggesting that consumption itself is to be avoided in order to experience genuine happiness. I enjoy the products of the world as much as the next person. The distinction between genuine happiness and the error trap of material consumption is the temporary pleasure these products provide and the fact that they are incapable of bringing us the genuine happiness we are seeking. They can certainly bring us pleasure by their novelty, variety, and uses, but they are things and by their very nature are incapable of providing us with the intimate, life-affirming qualities of genuine happiness.

The evidence that reveals the error trap of the proposition that says outside things bring us genuine happiness is that the more we act in alignment with this faulty premise, the further away we get from the genuine happiness we are seeking. Genuine happiness is not a function of anything external to us but begins inside us and expands through changes in our perceptions, feelings, beliefs, and actions.

When we encounter genuine happiness on the inside, regardless of our external situation, we will continue to experience it. Conversely, if we are unhappy on the inside, then no amount of external abundance will change our internal experience. The genuine happiness we desire is like a reservoir of intimacy, connection, appreciation, and gratitude. It reflects our sense of possessing a life of worth, meaning, purpose, and value. It instils in us a sense that despite all the confusion and suffering in the world, we retain the capacity to encounter and extend loving kindness in our lives and the lives of everyone we touch. Through intimate (self-revealing), loving engagement, we gain the confidence to know that regardless of external conditions, we have acquired a conscious relationship with Unconditional Love who seeks only to multiply Itself in our lives and, through us, the world.

Genuine happiness is one expression of unconditional love, and it is through extending this unconditionally loving energy into the world that we generate the quality of genuine happiness that is our birthright as spiritual beings having a human experience.

In nurturing our experience of genuine happiness, we discover that it begins to expand. With this expansion, the quality of our life improves. Getting more deeply and consciously in touch with our own unconditionally loving nature, and then extending this loving energy into the world, we soon notice our capacity to access and express feelings of gratitude, appreciation, and joy. With conscious attention to cultivating genuine happiness on the inside we soon discover that these multifariously wonderful facets of genuine happiness occur more frequently and begin to occupy a larger portion of our daily experience. Looking within is the secret and solution to achieving the genuine happiness we desire, and the more we focus on it, the less we feel the pull from the outside world telling us what it thinks we need in order to be happy.

Having recovered our capacity to experience genuine happiness from the inside out, we discover that other qualities within us begin to clamour for attention. These qualities are the unique expressions of unconditional love that we are singularly capable of bringing to life in the world. Each of us shares the common lineage of the same universe yet, like wild flowers in a mountain meadow, each of us is utterly unique in how the Universe expresses Itself through us. Identifying and nurturing this unique expression is how we thank the Universe for the gift of life we have received from It. With this goal in mind, we now shift our attention to the third stage of reclaiming the life we lost along the way. This stage invites the conscious development and realization of our unique and inherent potential, which is achieved by identifying and bringing our unique gifts to life.

EXPANDING SELF-AWARENESS

1. Thinking about a time in my life when I was genuinely happy, what was the source of my happiness?

2. Based on what I've learned about experiencing genuine happiness through intimate connection with others, how can I bring more genuine happiness into my life?

3. How are my relationships and expectations of people, places, and things outside of me changing as the result of accessing genuine happiness through authentic connection with others?

4. What is changing for me as I begin seeking genuine happiness inside myself rather than through external sources?

5. Based on my growing realization of the ways I can experience genuine happiness, what will I do differently to expand genuine happiness in my life?

APPLYING SELF-AWARENESS

Take a sheet of paper and draw a line down the middle of the page. On the left hand top of the page write: "Things that bring me pleasure." On the right hand top of the page write: "Things that bring me genuine happiness." After listing the things that bring you pleasure and genuine happiness, ask yourself the following questions.

1. What did I learn about pleasure and genuine happiness from this exercise?

2. How does my understanding of pleasure and genuine happiness change my perspective of what I want more of?

3. What emotions come up for me from this exercise?

4. Based on what I learned, what—if anything—will I change?

5. What do I hope these changes will do to improve the quality of my life?

PART THREE

BRINGING OUR GIFTS TO LIFE

CHAPTER SIXTEEN:

EVERYONE HAS A UNIQUE GIFT
TO OFFER THE WORLD

"There is more to us than we know. If we can be made to see it, perhaps, for the rest of our lives, we will be unwilling to settle for less."
— *Kurt Hahn (1886-1974)*

When I think about the state of the world I sometimes feel overwhelmed. There is so much suffering and heartache, and I feel so powerless to change it. I am aware of how fortunate I am to be living where I do, with a healthy body and a functioning mind, and I wonder at the apparent injustice of people confronting terrible conditions—not of their own making—who face tremendous hurdles on their journey to secure a better quality of life for themselves and the people they love.

I don't pretend to know why we find ourselves in such radically different circumstances, and how this makes sense at some universal level. It will be for someone far smarter and wiser than me to unravel this mystery. What I do know is that all of us need to make sense of our lives within the context of the world. Since I believe we are spiritual beings having a human experience, and the goal of our life is to put our ego consciousness in the service of Unconditional Love, then regardless of conditions the question remains the same: "How do we experience and express Unconditional Love in the circumstances we find ourselves in?"

There are as many forms of loving expression as there are people on the planet. Each of us is situated in a particular place and with particular resources, skills, and abilities that can be offered to the service of Unconditional Love. While I am only one person, I am one person, and while I cannot address all the challenges that impact humanity, I can offer my limited services in the capacity of which I am capable. This is how we can individually respond to the world. This is how we can invite and extend Unconditional Love into the world. Rather than becoming overwhelmed by the complexity of the world, every day we can ask: "How can I best serve Unconditional Love today?"

The way each of us can most effectively bring our gifts into the world is to put our gifts in the service of the God of our understanding, praying for the knowledge and wisdom to extend them—to the best of our ability—in whatever capacity our Higher Power chooses. We can trust that whatever our contributions are, they are precisely the gifts required to extend Unconditional Love into the world.

Creating a more unconditionally loving world begins by becoming more consciously loving beings. Gandhi said: "We must be the change we wish to see in the world." So the question becomes: "How do we become the change we wish to see in the world?" We do this by awakening and extending the beauty, wonder, and power of our unconditionally loving nature, in partnership with the God of our understanding, into the world. We make this choice concrete by doing everything in our power to bring our gifts into the world, each in our individual and utterly unique ways. As we discover what our unique gifts are, we begin to extend and experience the qualities that support the development and wellbeing of ourselves and those we encounter on our journey.

There is an old axiom that says: to keep it, we need to give it away; to be understood, start by understanding others; to be forgiven, extend forgiveness; to be honoured, honour others first; to experience abundance, share your good fortune; to be successful, help others succeed; to be an effective leader, serve others; to tell your story, listen to someone else's; to receive love, dignity, respect, and compassion, extend these qualities to everyone you meet.

Imagine how the world would improve if we each made a commitment to extend to others the qualities and characteristics we value and appreciate most. We don't need to save the world; all we need to do is become more loving and compassionate to those directly in front of us. As we extend more love and compassion into the lives of those we touch, they in turn are more inclined to do the same. This isn't rocket science; it's basic human nature. When we are treated kindly, we feel good and this feeling spills over into our interactions with others. In the same way, if we are treated unkindly, we feel upset and that feeling spills over, too.

The changes we desire in the world begin with us. To the degree we extend Unconditional Love into the world, that loving energy expands far beyond us. Like the ripples in a pond when we drop a rock in the water, they continue expanding outwards in all directions. To paraphrase Gandhi, if you would change the world, change yourself and inspire the world to change. No one else can bring about the changes you alone are capable of generating in your life. And as these changes expand within you, everything you do will change in kind. As you become more consciously loving, your behaviours become more loving. You will find love multiplying in your life, in the lives of everyone you touch, in the lives of everyone they touch, and so on. This is why your contribution is irreplaceable. Only you can share Unconditional Love the way you can, and should you choose not to share your unique expressions of Unconditional Love, then they will be lost to the world. Let us consider more concretely how to access these unique gifts that offer so much promise.

ACCESSING OUR GIFTS

We are more than we imagined. Having lived with the self-limiting ideas about who we think we are for too long, our challenge is exploring ways we might live more fully. This starts by identifying and incorporating the qualities and characteristics we admire and respect in others into our own lives. Identifying these qualities and characteristics, and discovering ways to access and express them, is the starting point for bringing our unique, God-given talents and abilities to life so that we, and everyone we touch, can experience greater happiness through sharing our gifts.

So how do we identify our unique gifts? One of the easiest ways is to think about the qualities and characteristics (QCs) we admire in others. The fact that we admire them is a sure sign that these QCs reflect some aspect of our own talents, abilities, and nature. For example, one of the people I respect is Gregory Peck for the way he treated people with courtesy, dignity, and respect. The fact that I am attracted to these qualities shows me that courtesy, dignity, and respect are important qualities that I want to reflect in my interactions with others. This realization has a profound impact on the way I consciously choose to relate to others and significantly enhances the quality of those relationships.

The QCs we admire and respect in others are evidence that these same QCs reside within us. If these QCs weren't part of our nature, we wouldn't be attracted to them. The more QCs we become aware of, the more gifts we have to bring into our own lives and the lives of everyone we touch.

The experience of living a meaningful life comes from believing we have something of value to bring to the world. An effective way of bringing our value to the world is to identify the QCs we admire and respect, and then figure out ways of expressing them in our own unique ways. If you admire psychologists, perhaps you can find a way of helping other people who are struggling in life. You might become a teacher or a crisis-line volunteer. If you love animals, you might become an animal trainer or work for the SPCA. If you love music, you might learn to play a musical instrument or become a DJ. If you respect people who engage in intellectual conversations, perhaps you will go to school and study the subjects that interest you. Perhaps you will form a club where people who share similar interests come to discuss their latest insights. The list is virtually endless. By identifying what we admire and respect, we gain insight into our life energy and passions. Bringing these qualities and interests into the world enriches our own lives and the lives of everyone we touch.

Here are some questions that may help you access the QCs you possess but have not yet realized:

- What do I love to do?

- What is it about the things I love to do that gives me pleasure, a sense of satisfaction and accomplishment?

- What are my skills, talents, and interests?

- If my work reflected my gifts, and there were no limitations, what would I do for a living?

As you begin experimenting with bringing your QCs to life, don't worry if it takes you time figuring out the most effective ways of expressing them. For some of us, if we can't do something perfectly the first time, we don't want to attempt it at all. This decision would be a great loss to you and the world, as both will benefit from your patient testing and practice of your newfound passions. As Voltaire noted, "Sometimes the best is the enemy of the better." Progress, not perfection, is the goal of this aspect of personal development. The expanding sense of meaning and value you will experience is not determined by how *well* you express your QCs but by the fact that you *are* expressing them.

Notice how your experiences change as you begin putting your positive QCs into action. As the quality of your life experience improves, keep asking yourself: "How can I bring more of my lost or hidden QCs into my life so everyone—including me—can benefit from them?"

Don't worry about doing this for the rest of your life. Focus on bringing as many of your QCs into your life and the lives of those you touch on a daily basis. Making lifelong commitments is another error trap of our ego. We can't live the rest of our life today. All we can live is one moment, and then the next, and the next. Take it one day at a time, and if you find yourself drifting back into ego-domination, simply become aware of it and gently realign your consciousness back to Unconditional Love. There is no need for judgement or recrimination, just a gentle shifting back to the alignment that brings you a better life experience.

Finally, don't judge yourself harshly for not actively using all the qualities and characteristics you identify as being important to you. Growth takes time, and you have the rest of your life to explore and develop a whole range of talents and abilities. As John Harricharan noted, "growth and learning take time. Sometimes what is gained in speed is lost in strength. Build strong at your own pace." With this healthy caution in mind, we can shift our attention to exploring more fully the various ways in which we can express our emerging gifts.

EXPRESSING OUR GIFTS

The rationale for expressing our gifts is simple: we are happier and more fulfilled when we do. As noted above, the process of expressing our gifts begins by identifying the qualities and characteristics we admire and respect in other people. Our next step is to review what we're good at and what we enjoy putting our time and effort into. Then we identify ways to bring these desirable qualities and characteristics into our lives more. The purpose of this process is to dig deeper to find ways of expressing in our own unique ways the qualities and characteristics we admire. For example, one of the qualities I really admire in people is their willingness to help others reach their potential. To reflect this quality in my own life, I decided to think about everyone I interact with. I became curious about ways to support them in achieving their potential. I started by asking them questions about what they felt they were good at. What did they want to accomplish? What hobbies, interests, and activities did they enjoy? What is it about those activities that gave them pleasure and a sense of accomplishment? What gave them a sense of pride? What did they think would be necessary to begin moving in the direction of accomplishing their desires more effectively?

Besides asking questions to help them identify their values and goals, I explored how they might honour the qualities and characteristics they admired and respected in others. I became a sounding board for them. I got to hear their thinking out loud. By looking at what they were doing and what they wanted to do, from as many angles as possible, they were able to identify ways that they could develop and express their unique gifts. I offered encouragement and support for their efforts. When they started to beat themselves up for their perceived lack of progress, I reminded them that every journey begins with the first step. Easy does it, but do it. The goal wasn't instant results, I suggested. Rather, a gradual and persistent desire to achieve their goals would enable them to enjoy the journey.

We gain the quality of life we are seeking through the positive feelings we experience when engaged in a worthwhile activity. When focused on living as fully as possible, we renew our sense of purpose, meaning, and excitement. It's like the feeling we get when we are doing something we really want to do—time flies, we feel energized, and we are genuinely happy. This is the real goal of living as fully and wholly as possible. The outcome isn't nearly as important as the process where we move thoughtfully and purposefully through our day engaged in activities that reflect what we care about most.

If you love helping people reach their potential, and you honour this passion by helping others explore ways of bringing their potential to life, if you celebrate every step they take towards increasing their sense of self-worth, dignity, and enthusiasm, then you will experience genuine happiness through every stage of their journey.

Whether we achieve everything we set out to is far less important than the countless moments of self-worth and satisfaction we collect every time we extend our unique gifts. Each act is rewarded with growing optimism that we are more competent than we imagined. We are free and capable of finding ways to share our gifts, make our unique contributions, and feel truly alive with possibilities for new discoveries and experiences.

Our sense of personal accomplishment comes from acting on our gifts. Living our gifts allows us to feel fully alive, and the gratitude and genuine happiness that flows from this daily investment is what we've been seeking. It comes from the inside out. It is the genuine happiness of honouring the value of our own life and seeing our gifts extending through us into the world.

Our purpose is to discover our unique gifts and then develop and extend them into our lives and the lives of everyone we touch. This is how we enhance our experience of self-worth, purpose, meaning, and genuine happiness. Bringing our unique interests, skills, and talents into the world is the greatest gift we can give to the world and ourselves.

I would like to share a short story by Les Brown that I came across many years ago. It powerfully summarizes the cost of holding our gifts inside us.

An elderly man, in the final days of his life, is lying in bed alone. He awakens to see a large group of people clustered around his bed. Their faces are loving, but sad. Confused, the old man smiles weakly and whispers, "You must be my childhood friends come to say good-bye. I am so grateful."

Moving closer, the tallest figure gently grasps the old man's hand and replies, "Yes, we are your best and oldest friends, but long ago you abandoned us. For we are the unfulfilled promises of your youth. We are the unrealized hopes, dreams, and plans that you once felt deeply in your heart, but never pursued. We are the unique talents that you never refined, the special gifts you never discovered. Old friend, we have not come to comfort you but to die with you.

Each of us expresses our QCs differently. This is where our uniqueness really shines. While we all arise from the same unconditionally loving source, the way we express it is unique. There has never been—nor will there ever be—another you. In the entire universe, you are a unique manifestation of Unconditional Love. Your way of expressing love is irreplaceable! As you learn how to encounter your own loving nature and then extend it into your life and the lives of everyone you touch, you will begin to experience the beauty, wonder, and joy of Unconditional Love encountering Itself consciously in the world through you. This is our destiny, and the fulfillment of that destiny is entirely up to each of us since Unconditional Love will never violate our right to reject our own deepest identity. *The choice is entirely up to us!*

Every minute of every day we can choose to exercise our unique talents, skills, and abilities. Choosing to bring our gifts into our lives and the lives of those we touch increases our experience of self-respect, dignity, and genuine happiness. Every minute of every day we are also free to change our minds. Choosing not to live our gifts causes us to retreat into a half-lived life of frustration, disappointment, and suffering. Should the internal voices of judgement or criticism suggest that the gifts you have to share with the world are insignificant, know that this is another error trap that assumes the Universe weighs and measures our gifts by some arbitrary scale of value. In the next chapter we will see why this assumption is absurd and lay to rest the notion that size and scale of contribution has any relevance to its value.

EXPANDING SELF-AWARENESS

1. Do I recognize that the reason I am drawn to specific qualities and characteristics (QCs) is because they reflect the same QCs within me?

2. Am I willing to test and practice these emerging QCs without demanding perfection?

3. How will I begin to access and develop the QCs I respect and admire to better express my gifts and experience greater meaning in my life?

4. What stories am I telling myself that undermine my confidence and/or ability to develop my interests, skills, and talents?

5. How can I more effectively share my gifts with others at work, at home, and in the community?

APPLYING SELF-AWARENESS

Take a sheet of paper and draw a line down the middle of the page. On the left hand top of the page write: "The QCs I admire and respect in others." On the right hand top of the page write: "QCs I admire and respect in myself." Compare both lists and identify QCs in others that are not present in the list of yourself. Then answer the following questions.

1. What did I learn about the QCs I admire and respect in others?

2. How many of these QCs did I identify in myself?

3. What are some of the ways I might express these QCs?

4. How does my understanding of the QCs I admire and respect in others change my perspective on expanding them in my own life?

5. How can I begin to express these gifts in my personal and professional life?

6. How will making these changes enable me to increase the gifts I can contribute to the world?

7. What emotions come up for me from this exercise?

8. Based on what I learned, what—if anything—will I change?

9. What do I hope these changes will do to improve my quality of life?

CHAPTER SEVENTEEN:

THERE ARE NO DEGREES OF LOVING-KINDNESS

In the same way that the world needs plumbers and carpenters as much as it needs philosophers and teachers, each of us was born to add our unique gifts to the world. No gift is better or worse, more or less worthy. Each contribution, no matter how big or small, whether between two strangers or encompassing the globe, is part of the mosaic that adds to the richness and wellbeing of us all.

In keeping with the nature of our individual contributions to the world, I have frequently heard people voice the concern that they don't believe their small acts of kindness make any real difference. Differences, they say, only matter when they are big enough to impact a significant number of people, so how does their small deed matter in the grand scheme of things? This, to me, is an understandable leap of logic, but one that is completely inaccurate. Can any act of genuine loving kindness be legitimately evaluated as more or less loving based on its form or size? When one human being reaches out to another in the spirit of loving kindness is that act any less loving because it is focused on one individual rather than a hundred? I believe this error in perception about size equalling worth is a carryover from the same logic that supposes a larger and more expensive gift as better than a smaller less expensive one. Doesn't the value of any gift depend on the spirit in which it is given? The smallest gift given with love is more life-affirming than the most extravagant gift given out of a sense of duty or guilt. Any gift given in love enriches the giver and the receiver while expanding the flow of unconditional love.

I remember looking out the window in my kitchen. My 10-year-old son walked up behind me and gave me a hug. I asked him why he did that, and he said: "You just looked like you needed a hug," and then he walked away. By any standard of comparison, it might seem a very small gift. Years later, the impact of that simple act of loving kindness continues to resonate in my life. My son taught me just how powerful the smallest act of loving kindness and consideration can have in a person's life. I came to realize through many other such moments, and in hearing similar stories from others, that the power of love is such that any act has the potential to transform a life.

It seems only fitting that the Universe wouldn't require extravagant demonstrations of love to qualify as truly loving acts since many of us do not live extravagant lives. Most of our interactions are with a relatively small number of people and unfold in unspectacular ways. The impact of these loving encounters, however, isn't diminished by the scale of the act; the impact is determined by the sincerity of the gesture. The Universe doesn't distinguish degrees of loving kindness. Every act is either loving or it's not. Every action born out of loving intention multiplies love.

If you ever find yourself questioning the value of the smallest act of loving kindness, and wonder if it truly makes a difference, know that Unconditional Love smiles whenever and wherever It encounters Itself, because Its only intention is to multiply Itself. A single drop of seawater contains within it the whole mystery of the ocean, and the ocean achieves its grandeur from every drop of water within it. Both are aspects of the same thing, and both benefit from their shared interaction.

EXPANDING SELF-AWARENESS

1. Do I recognize that every act of loving kindness, regardless of its size, adds Unconditional Love to the world?

2. In what ways have I discovered that every act of genuine love counts?

3. How have small or random acts of love positively impacted my life?

4. Understanding that the loving intention behind any gift is more powerful than the size of the gift, do I recognize that every act of loving kindness is equal in value?

5. Knowing that every loving action extends Unconditional Love into the world, what small and simple ways can I extend Unconditional Love in my life and the lives of those I touch?

APPLYING SELF-AWARENESS

On a sheet of paper, write down small acts of kindness you have experienced or extended to yourself and others. When you've finished writing, answer the following questions.

1. What did I learn about the variety of ways I can extend small acts of kindness into the world?

2. How does my understanding and appreciation of the power of small acts of kindness change my perspective on their value?

3. What emotions come up for me from this exercise?

4. Based on what I learned, what—if anything—will I change?

5. What do I hope these changes will do to improve the quality of my life?

CHAPTER EIGHTEEN:

WE ARE MORE AMAZING THAN WE IMAGINE

I know that despite everything you've read up to now you may still think that you don't deserve the unconditional love described in this book and/ or that you can't identify with your own unconditionally loving nature. I understand how much resistance you may be encountering with these suggestions as well as all the reasons your ego is giving you for why they don't apply to you. But I promise you that to the extent you attempt to consciously connect with your unconditionally loving nature, you will experience and recover the unconditional love that is your deepest truth and identity. Your longing for love proves that love is woven into the fabric of your nature. It is your decision to consciously live from your unconditionally loving nature that increases your capacity to extend and encounter unconditional love in your life.

When I started this journey 37 years ago, I thought I was probably insane, because anybody who caused so much heartache and disappointment without intending to must be insane. I believed I would be doing the world a favour if I simply disappeared and died. I think if I could have come up with a plan to kill myself without it hurting, I would have done so. Instead, in utter desperation, I sought out a 12-step program. Never in my wildest dreams could I have imagined how that decision would positively impact my life.

I started this journey believing that I was a piece of human garbage. For reasons beyond my understanding, I concluded that I didn't possess the qualities and characteristics necessary to succeed in the world. I believed I had nothing to offer the world but disappointment and pain. I couldn't see how things would ever change. This is the story I was telling myself. It was a reasonable story, based on my track record at the time, but I discovered it wasn't the whole story.

Unbeknownst to me there was another aspect to myself that I didn't know anything about. It was a stubborn spark of life energy willing me not to kill myself. It wanted to live. In time I came to understand that this spark of life energy was Unconditional Love trying to wake me up from the error traps and faulty mental models that were dominating my life. As the fog started to lift, I came to realize that I did want to live. I also discovered that what I really longed for was to be someone other people could love and respect—someone people wanted in their lives. In time, all of my longings were satisfied. I came to experience a quality of life that I never imagined possible, and the journey to the life I am so blessed to be living today began when I became willing to consider that I wasn't a piece of human garbage but a frightened, wounded human desperately seeking love, safety, acceptance, and authentic connection with others.

In receiving love, acceptance, and authentic connection through my recovery community, I began to encounter these same qualities within myself. I realized that to nurture these gifts, I needed to give them away to others. By extending loving kindness into the lives of others, more loving kindness came into my life. Throughout the process, the story I told about myself began to change. I no longer believed I was worthless. I came to realize that I had been sick and deeply confused about the person I thought I was. With the compassionate support and encouragement of loving strangers, I began to experience my own capacity for unconditional love. The net effect was a profound transformation in my life experience.

I have witnessed this transformation thousands of times with people from every walk of life. This transformation isn't unique to particular people; it occurs every time someone reaches out for help and encounters unconditional love, acceptance, and authentic connection. There is nothing unique about them or me. This transformation is available to anyone willing to challenge the story they believe about everything they lack, to anyone willing to consider that the story may appear reasonable but is, in truth, incomplete.

Whatever story you're telling yourself, it is not fully written. The same stubborn spark of life energy is willing you to wake up and discover that you too have Unconditional Love waiting patiently to express Itself through you. The misguided belief that you are inadequate, that you are different, or that you are powerless to change the direction of your life is the faulty assumption you need to move beyond. It is an error trap you need to challenge, because it simply isn't accurate.

You are more amazing than you can imagine. You have no idea how many lives you are going to impact on your journey, but I can assure you that it will be many. The key to the life you want to live begins with the willingness to consider that your deepest nature is Unconditional Love. By consciously trying to encounter and express the tiniest degree of Unconditional Love towards yourself and others, things will begin to change. One morning you will discover that you appreciate your life and you appreciate yourself. The dark shadows that overwhelmed you for so long will fade away under the light of your conscious choice to live each day with as much unconditional love, gratitude, and authentic connection as you can.

Each of us matters. Each of us possesses unique gifts, and as long as we are on this earth, our challenge and opportunity is to realize our unique potential by doing everything in our power to extend our gifts into our lives and the lives of everyone we touch.

I pray you come to know how lovable you really are and come to realize that the Universe is constantly bringing people, events, and things into your life to assist you on your journey of discovering and recovering the beauty, wonder, and power of your own unconditionally loving nature. God works through people. Find people who are loving, and listen to what they have to say. Find people who are living the life you want to live, and ask them how they do it. The more you reach out to Unconditional Love, the more Unconditional Love will reach out to you. The choice is absolutely and exclusively yours!

You are not your secrets. You are not what you have done to others, and you are not what others have done to you. The life you live is a direct reflection of the choices you make today. Regardless of what happened in your past, today you are free to become curious about the life you are living and the life you want to live. Curiosity encourages willingness, and willingness invites us to consider alternatives to the "certainties" we have been operating under. The only certainty we have is the certainty that the way we see the world and ourselves determines the choices we make. The sum of these choices creates our life experience. Changing our experience begins with changing our perceptions. We cannot control the conditions we encounter, but we can control our responses to them. Inviting

Unconditional Love to assist us in making more loving responses to the world changes our life, and the lives of everyone we touch, in the most amazing and life-enhancing ways.

I will end this chapter with the four immeasurable thoughts of Buddhism that I invite you to silently recite towards everyone you encounter throughout your day. This practice will enhance your experience of compassion, acceptance, and gratitude. As a consequence of expanding your conscious relationship with these qualities, you will encounter greater peace, joy, and abundance in your life as you extend them towards all other beings.

> *May you have happiness and the causes of happiness;*
> *May you be free from suffering and the causes of suffering;*
> *May you never be separated from the happiness that knows no suffering;*
> *May you live in equanimity, free from attachment and aversion.*
> — *(Rinpoche, 2014, p. 1)*

This brings us to the final stage of our journey: The World Beyond. It is now time to turn our attention towards considering the most effective ways of sharing our gifts with the world.

EXPANDING SELF-AWARENESS

1. Do I believe that I am inadequate or that I am incapable of letting my light shine?

2. Am I willing to challenge the story I've been telling myself about me?

3. Am I willing to believe that I am more than what I have done to others or what others have done to me?

4. What do I risk if I let my fears stop me from bringing my gifts into my life and the lives of others?

5. What do I gain by choosing to believe that I have more unconditional love to offer than what I have believed until now?

APPLYING SELF-AWARENESS

On a sheet of paper, write down the thoughts about yourself that undermine your willingness to receive love, understanding, and compassion from yourself and others. Then answer the following questions.

1. What did I learn about the thoughts that undermine my willingness to receive love, understanding, and compassion?

2. How does understanding these self-limiting thoughts change my perspective on receiving more love, understanding, and compassion?

3. What emotions come up for me from this exercise?

4. Based on what I learned, what—if anything—will I change?

5. What do I hope these changes will do to improve the quality of my life?

PART FOUR

THE WORLD BEYOND

CHAPTER NINETEEN:

HEALING THE WOUNDS IN OUR PAST

Having discovered that we are more than the story we have been telling ourselves all these years, having regained the capacity to access our uncon-ditionally loving nature, and having begun to express this nature through identifying the unique gifts we have to offer, we turn to the final stage of our journey: to reclaim the life we lost along the way, which occurred long ago when our ego first decided it knew the way we needed to live in order to get the love, safety, acceptance, and authentic connection we need to thrive.

To effectively share our gifts with the world, we need to make peace with the world. Making peace starts with healing the wounds we have created in our past. It is this healing process that enables us to embrace the world in a way that has eluded us up until now. So long as we believe that there are people to whom we owe amends, we are going to suffer. While the prospect of making amends can be difficult and frightening, our ability to achieve a more life-affirming and internally peaceful experience with the world depends on our willingness to redress the wrongs we perceive we've done to others and to ourselves. The nature of our amends will vary depending on our particular circumstances. Some of those we've harmed may have moved away or passed away. In this case, all we can do is humbly ask our Higher Power to accept, on their behalf, our sincere amends.

For those still living and within range of contact, every effort needs to be made to contact them to express sincere regret for the harms we have done them (unless doing so would cause further harm, for example: apologizing to a husband for an affair with his wife while they are still married and he knows nothing about the affair). There is no substitute for making face-to-face amends, but if circumstances don't permit it, a letter or a phone call will suffice—anything that enables us to address past errors so we can let go of them once and for all.

The outcome of these amends is often pleasantly surprising and can set the stage for a newfound relationship based on our willingness to admit our errors and change our approach to our fellows going forward. Often family relationships and past friendships are restored in new and rewarding ways. Sometimes we are surprised to discover that when making our amends to others, they too feel the need to make amends to us. When regrettable situations occur between people, each person carries within them the wounds—received and inflicted—and both benefit from owning their part in the situation, apologizing for it, and choosing not to do the same thing again.

Regardless of the response we get, the benefit to us arises from our genuine desire to set the record straight, to apologize for any wrongs we have committed, and to make a decision to change our behaviours going forward. We gain the benefits of making our amends regardless of how our amends are received. We are responsible for our output, not the outcome. That is between them and their Higher Power. Ultimately the sincerity of our amends can best be demonstrated by not behaving the same way in the future.

The benefits of making amends extends much further than apologizing for wrongs we've committed against others; it makes space in our heart and mind for new feelings, thoughts, and actions to arise. So long as we hold onto unresolved conflicts within, they continue to fester and poison our relationship with ourselves and with others. It also hurts our relationship with our Higher Power, not because our Higher Power withholds love but because we can't accept unconditional love so long as we believe we don't deserve it.

When it comes to making amends to ourselves, we need to recognize that we are probably our own harshest critics and frequently say things we wouldn't dream of saying to anyone else. Where we might be willing to give someone else the benefit of the doubt, or overlook their shortcomings, with ourselves we are merciless. We rail against our choices and then wonder why our sense of self-esteem is so tattered and fragile. Being on the receiving end of so much self-criticism, is it any wonder we feel unworthy of receiving love?

We can do ourselves the greatest possible service by recognizing that we too are doing the best we can with the mental models and resources we have at our disposal. While we can accept that we have made ineffective choices in the past, we also know that we are open to learning from them. We remember that learning comes from trial and error, and we—like everyone else—didn't come into this life with an owner's manual. Our responsibility to ourselves is to pay attention to our thoughts and actions, observe the consequences, and then determine if the consequences are undesirable. In the future when we face similar situations, we are free to make different choices that produce more effective results. This is how we learn and grow.

Beating ourselves up before compassionately evaluating our thoughts and actions actually slows the learning process down, because to avoid the suffering we inflict on ourselves we avoid looking at the situation we are trying to evaluate. A critical step in our growth is to forgive ourselves when we make a mistake. No one sets out to deliberately screw up. While our actions may have created terrible consequences, those consequences were not our intention. We acted or reacted only to discover after-the-fact that the outcome was not what we intended or desired. This is when we need to forgive ourselves for failing to achieve our intended results. By forgiving ourselves, we are able to compassionately review our actions and determine how we can respond more effectively in the future.

It's easier to be compassionate than self-compassionate. It's easier to forgive than be forgiven. It's easier to love another than it is to love ourselves. Why is that, I wonder?

- Is it possible that we don't believe we deserve compassion, forgiveness, and love?

- Is it possible that we believe if people really knew our secrets, they would find us so despicable that they too would withhold compassion, forgiveness, and love?

- Do we resist taking the risk of exposing our deepest secrets for fear that our worst suspicions about ourselves will be confirmed by others proving once and for all that we really are undeserving of compassion, forgiveness, and love?

What a diabolical error trap! The only way we can receive compassion, forgiveness, and love from others is if we expose our secrets to their scrutiny and risk rejection. On the other hand, by not exposing ourselves to their scrutiny, we ensure that we cannot receive their compassion, forgiveness, and love. By refusing to share what we truly believe about ourselves, any compassion, forgiveness, and love they extend us must be rejected since they don't really know who they are loving and forgiving.

Before we can accept compassion, forgiveness, and love from others we must be willing to accept it from ourselves. We must be willing to extend towards ourselves the same consideration we are willing to extend towards others. We are human. We are imperfect. We have made mistakes in the past and will make mistakes in the future. That doesn't make us unforgivable or undeserving of compassion and love. It simply means that everything we did made perfect sense at the time. With the benefit of hindsight, and the willingness to learn from our mistakes, we are seeking another chance to respond more effectively in the future. If we are able to give others this chance, is it not simple fairness that we give ourselves the same chance?

Practicing self-compassion, self-forgiveness, and self-love is the key to discovery, growth, wisdom, and recovery. It is how we heal the wounds of the past and open the door to different beliefs and behaviours that will benefit us and everyone we touch.

The most powerful amends we can make is the amends we extend to ourselves. As we begin to heal from our self-inflicted wounds of self-criticism, self-loathing, and self-recrimination, we open ourselves up to encountering the compassion, forgiveness, and unconditional love that lives within us, waiting patiently for us to invite it into our life. We can extend it to ourselves, not because we believe we can ever be perfect but precisely because of our imperfection. Like everyone else, we need compassion, forgiveness, and unconditional love to help us grow into the people we are capable of becoming. As Goethe noted, "If we treat people as they are, we make them worse. But if we treat people as if they were what they are capable of becoming, we help them become it." This applies to us as much as it applies to everyone else.

With all my heart I implore you to extend self-compassion, self-forgiveness, and loving kindness into your own life so you can begin to benefit from the healing such an orientation provides. From this place of self-acceptance, self-compassion, and loving kindness, you will be amazed at your capacity to extend and encounter these qualities in your interactions with the world, in particular with those who have hurt you.

Your ability to forgive others is a critically important and achievable next step in your journey, because as the love within you begins to expand you realize that your resistance to self-forgiveness has trapped you in pain and guilt. It has also prevented you from releasing the pain you continue to experience from the unearned suffering you've endured at the hands of others. To release the pain we must decide to let go of our resistance to forgiveness. To the extent we achieve this, space is created within us that we can fill with compassion, empathy, and loving kindness. Making amends and forgiveness are two sides of the same coin. They both enable us to significantly improve the quality of our lives and the lives of those we touch by releasing our pain, shame, guilt, and resentments. How we go about forgiving others for the unearned suffering they inflicted on us is the next order of business.

FORGIVING OTHERS

The path of forgiving others and healing the wounds we've suffered is clearly marked. So long as we hold on to anger, resentment, and hostility towards someone we continue to suffer. Forgiving others is not about approving their actions. Forgiveness is about letting go of the internal anger that is poisoning our peace of mind. When we forgive someone, what we are actually doing is recognizing that their actions hurt us once while our continued inability to release our anger and resentment is hurting us over and over again. Long after the event we can still suffer by re-living and re-hating the perpetrator.

Forgiveness is about self-healing and self-care. The easiest way to forgive someone is to pray for their wellbeing. As ridiculous as this sounds, the fact remains that when we pray for their wellbeing it becomes less and less possible to continue to maintain the same level of hostility towards them. Praying for them releases the anger within us.

What about fairness? What about justice? How can we let them get away with what they did? These reactions are typical of the resistance we encounter when we are asked to forgive someone. And these are perfectly valid questions. It does seem unfair to forgive without receiving some kind of restitution. The question I pose to you is: how do you know they got away without suffering for their actions?

Reverse the rolls for a moment and consider the challenge of making amends described earlier. Each of us has unjustly suffered and each of us has inflicted unjust suffering on others. When we caused others to suffer, did we not also suffer? Did we really get away with our unjust behaviours? Even though the other person has no way of knowing how we suffered from guilt, remorse, regret, shame, etc., when we unjustly hurt someone, we suffered too. Unjust suffering hurts everyone. What makes us think that the people who unjustly hurt us are not similarly suffering?

Buddha said, "If we knew the whole truth behind every situation, our only response would be compassion." When we think about the unjust harm we have caused others, what would we give to have them see our actions through the lens of compassion? Is this not what we secretly hope for when we are making our amends? Are those who have harmed us less deserving of the same compassion we yearn for from those we've harmed? Can we realistically accept compassion from others when we are unwilling to extend compassion towards those who have harmed us?

Forgiving others who have unjustly harmed us relieves us of the ongoing suffering we inflict on ourselves by holding onto our resentments. It also permits us to believe that we too are capable and deserving of being forgiven for the harms, intended or not, we have caused others. Forgiving is not forgetting. Forgiveness is about releasing the pain created by continuously re-experiencing the harm done to us. It is how we end our suffering.

Forgiving others helps us ensure we never harm another the way we were harmed. This is how we create a more loving world. If we can remember how it felt to be treated unjustly, we are more likely to behave justly towards others. In this way, injustice is converted from suffering to healing. Through forgiveness we become more compassionate because we accept that we all need forgiveness at some point in our lives. In the same way we hope that those we have harmed can forgive us and move beyond the unearned suffering we caused, we too are invited to grow in wisdom and compassion by letting go of the unearned suffering we have experienced.

When we are able to convert our suffering into greater compassion for our fellow human beings, our suffering becomes sacred. We, and the world, are redeemed by our compassion to forgive and to bring our insights— learned through pain—into the lives of everyone we touch.

Extending compassion invites compassion. Extending forgiveness invites forgiveness. Forgiving others frees us from the pain of re-living our suffering and frees us to experience greater peace in our lives. We are not compelled to make amends. We are not compelled to forgive. Yet it is only in making amends and forgiving that we are released from the pain of remorse and resentment. The choice is exclusively ours, and whichever choice we make, we and we alone will live with the consequences of suffering or redemption. Learning how to forgive is critical to our cultivation of compassion and serenity.

Beyond making amends and extending forgiveness, there are other more subtle changes we can make in relation to others that enable us to bring greater acceptance and tranquility into our lives. In the next chapter we will address one of these beneficial changes, that of reframing our understanding and orientation towards our opinions and the opinions of others. Gaining a more accurate understanding of the value and limitations of opinions can eliminate much distress and heartache. With this understanding, we will discover that opinions exert far more pressure on us than they should. With a simple reframe, they lose their disproportionate power to create division and dissention, and resume their proper role as evolving guides that help us make sense of our experience and the world beyond.

EXPANDING SELF-AWARENESS

1. Who do I need to make amends to?

2. What do I risk by not making these amends?

3. What price have I paid by holding onto my anger and resentments?

4. How might I more effectively bring my light into the world by forgiving others?

5. How might I more effectively bring my light into the world by forgiving myself?

APPLYING SELF-AWARENESS

Take a sheet of paper and draw a line down the middle of the page. On the left hand top of the page write: "People I owe an amends to." On the right hand top of the page write "People I need to forgive." Identify as many as you can think of under each heading and then ask yourself the following questions.

1. What do I need to do in order to make amends?

2. What is the risk of not making amends?

3. What do I need to do to forgive those who have harmed me?

4. What is the risk of not forgiving someone?

5. What do I believe will change for me when I complete my amends and forgive those who have harmed me?

6. What emotions come up for me from this exercise?

7. Based on what I learned, what—if anything—will I change?

8. What do I hope these changes will do to improve the quality of my life?

CHAPTER TWENTY:

EVERY OPINION IS VALID

When someone shares their opinion that the world is going to hell and points out all the terrible things they observed that proves their point, agree with them. Say: "You're absolutely right." And then add silently to yourself: "from your perspective." Someone with the opposite opinion could just as easily point out all the wonderful things they observed that proves that the world is bursting with loving kindness, and they too would be absolutely right—from their perspective. Both of these opinions are personal interpretations based on individual perspectives, so it is perfectly reasonable that both parties can hold opposite opinions and *both be right*.

Until people learn that every opinion is, in reality, a personal interpretation and not an objective fact, they frequently feel the need to prove their opinion is correct. They set about gathering support for their opinion by getting as many like-minded people as they can find to agree with them. When they've convinced a sufficient number of people, they offer this as "proof" that their opinion is correct. Of course, numerical strength doesn't add one ounce of logical weight to an opinion, so while they may have bolstered their confidence about it, they haven't "proven" anything.

This is important to remember when people challenge your opinions. Do not feel the need to prove your point or, more destructively, to prove them wrong. Your opinion doesn't require proof. The nature of an opinion is that it is valid because you believe it. This is how a person living in poverty can hold the opinion that they are on the road to achieving a better quality of life when all evidence suggests that they will follow the majority of their impoverished neighbours into a life of mere survival and premature death.

When someone holds a belief that they can secure a better quality of life, they act in harmony with that belief and they find things in their environment that validate their belief. As they focus on achieving greater abundance, they tend to recognize and exploit opportunities that make it possible for them to fulfill their belief. This is not an extraordinary occurrence. It is happening. Sometimes in little ways, sometimes in bigger ways, it is happening all the time. Every time someone holds a thought or perception and begins to act in harmony with it, a chain of events is set in motion, which advances the person in the direction of their dominant thoughts and beliefs.

If we reflect on the nature of our opinions, it becomes readily apparent that they are based on how we view the world around us. We literally construct our reality based on the particular lens we choose to view the world through. Imagine two people wearing different coloured glasses. One person is wearing a pair of red glasses and the other a pair of blue glasses. Both people look at a field of wild flowers. If you were to ask them to describe the field, each of them would see the field differently because each of them is perceiving it through different lenses. So which perspective is *right*? They both are viewed from their individual perspective. Another example is the story of two blind men who bumped into an elephant. One found the elephant's tail and the other the elephant's trunk. Each of the men was asked to describe the elephant. Their descriptions were radically different, yet each man insisted that his perspective was the correct one. So which of them was *right*? They both were from their particular perspective.

When we begin to understand that our opinions are actually based on a sliver of data we've selected from a vast pool of available information, then we begin to realize that our opinions are not objective facts but merely interpretations we've constructed based on the limited data we've chosen to pay attention to. What would happen if two people recognized that their positions or opinions were not objective facts but subjective interpretations based on how they each selected data to inform said positions or opinions? Knowing that each of them had equally valid opinions, might they be more willing to consider revising their own by choosing to view the situation from a broader perspective than either of them had viewed it before?

Recognizing that our opinions are based on limited information, and that new information may lead us to revise our earlier opinions, our willingness to explore different perspectives without getting defensive increases. As we become willing to step away from insisting that our opinions are *right* by recognizing they are actually subjective interpretations based on personal biases and worldviews, we are able to consider opinions from a broader and therefore more accurate perspective. Curiosity about other people's perspectives enables us to continue exploring, learning, and growing in knowledge and wisdom. Our goal is not to abandon our opinions but to subject them to a reasonable level of scrutiny, which invites a greater level of clarity that either supports or alters them. This is what humility looks like when it's applied to a behaviour.

Along with our opinions comes the well-intentioned temptation to offer them to others in the form of advice. And like our opinions, advice can generate as much dissention and heartache as it can harmony and healing. While the intention behind giving advice is generally loving, without the wisdom and humility to recognize the limitations and appropriateness of advice-giving, our best intentions can become a source of greater suffering than the suffering our advice was intended to relieve. With this in mind, let us give some thoughtful attention to this two-sided offering.

OFFERING ADVICE

Because all of us have opinions that make sense to us, we tend to offer them as advice when we think someone is in error or struggling. While this tendency is natural, it is often unhelpful. Each of us can probably remember how we felt when someone offered us advice we didn't ask for. We might argue with the advice-giver or tune them out because we weren't open to what they had to say. The same conditions apply to those we offer unsolicited advice to. Unless someone specifically asks for advice, chances are that any remarks we offer, however well-intentioned, will fall on deaf ears.

As a general rule, resist the temptation to offer advice that is not asked for. (In giving you this advice I'm acting on the principle of the writer's prerogative to presume that if you're reading this book, you have consented to receive the advice I am offering). To offer unsolicited advice is to impose on others our own point of view without permission, which is a subtle form of violence. When we find ourselves offering unsolicited advice we need to examine our motives. Are we trying to help by sharing our perspective? Are we trying to show the person where we think they've gone wrong? Are we hoping to alter their inaccurate perspective with a more accurate one?

By checking our motives before opening our mouths, we give ourselves the opportunity to learn more about ourselves. Since we know that we don't appreciate unsolicited advice, if we truly believe we have something of value to share with another, there are two effective ways to approach the situation.

(1) We can ask their permission to share our perspective with them, or

(2) We can wait until they ask for our opinion.

By holding off on giving our advice, we create the opportunity for the other person to become curious and open to our point of view. This is the prerequisite necessary for ideas to penetrate. Once someone has asked for our perspective, they have chosen to open their mind to our point of view. Whether they accept our point of view or not is none of our business. That is their journey of discovery. We have honoured ourselves and our relationship to them by waiting to be asked before sharing our perspective. That is our part. What they choose to do with our opinion is their part.

In the same way that we grow at our own rate, so too do we owe others the same courtesy. No one wants someone else's perspective shoved down their throat. When the thoughts, perceptions, and feelings they're holding no longer work for them, they will become curious about other perspectives. When that happens, they will reach out for guidance. Until then, leave them alone to work through their experiences the same way we reserve the right to test our perceptions to determine which ones are improving the quality of our lives and which are not.

EXPANDING SELF-AWARENESS

1. Since every opinion is a personal interpretation and not an objective fact, can I see how every opinion is equally valid even though it may be the opposite of my own?

2. Can I remember a time when I changed my opinion based on new information?

3. In what ways do my biases, preferences, and/or worldview influence the way I see things and the choices I make?

4. Am I willing to become teachable by loosening my grip on the opinions I feel strongly about? Am I willing to become more open-minded to alternative interpretations?

5. How much more effective might my advice be if I wait until it is asked for?

APPLYING SELF-AWARENESS

On a sheet of paper write: "If I was able to accept that every opinion is equally valid based on the perspective of the person holding it, I would..." Then complete the sentence ten times identifying how your perception of the opinions you and others hold might change. On the backside of the same sheet of paper write: "If I was able to resist the temptation to offer unsolicited advice to others I would..." Then complete the sentence ten times identifying how withholding you advice until it was requested might improve the quality of your interactions with others. Once you've written your sentences, answer the following questions.

1. What emotions come up for me from this exercise?

2. Based on what I learned, what—if anything—will I change?

3. What do I hope these changes will do to improve the quality of my life?

CHAPTER TWENTY-ONE:

UNIQUE AND THE SAME

For all our apparent differences, we are far more similar that we imagine. From our earliest years we learned that there are differences between us and everybody else. Different genders, families, interests, hobbies, talents, strengths, worldviews, etc. It is human nature to seek out and associate with those we have something in common with, and to generally ignore those who we don't have things in common with. On the basis of these similarities and differences, it is little wonder that we tend to move towards some people and away from others. We don't feel any particular hostility towards those we avoid; it's just that we don't really have anything in common with them, so there's less incentive to interact. Our professional associations and other distinctions further reinforce this situation. If we're well educated, we tend to associate with similarly educated people. If we're wealthy, we tend to live around and associate with other wealthy people, and so on.

You can imagine my surprise when I found myself in a room full of people who, by the standards of differences and similarities, had almost nothing in common expect their individual and collective desire to recover from an incurable disease. Now it wouldn't be extraordinary to imagine that people who share a similar fate might be thrown together and, for the duration of their common threat, form supportive relationships that might not otherwise occur if it weren't for said threat. People sharing a lifeboat after a shipwreck, for example, might form supportive relationships until they reach safety. The surprise for me with this recovery community was to discover that long after our common threat had been addressed, many of these people continued to grow and develop their friendships and, in many instances, became very close. This was a real curiosity to my belief system. If people associated with each other because of their similarities, and these individuals no longer shared a common threat, then how was it possible for them to continue to grow their friendship? On what basis was their friendship sustained?

What I observed was that these people came from very different backgrounds—their levels of education were vastly different; their lifestyles didn't appear compatible nor did they contain sufficient similarities to support a friendship—yet here they were in these deeply fulfilling relationships. I had to re-examine my assumptions. I knew I must have been missing something. So I decided to break it down. I observed people from different backgrounds, ages, cultures, genders, socio-economic levels, educational levels, talents, and interests, setting aside all their differences so I looked to identify what they shared in common out of which a lasting friendship could be established and sustained.

What they shared in common, I discovered, was their human yearnings. Regardless of their superficial differences, they ultimately desired the same things. First and foremost, they yearned to experience genuine happiness and to reduce their suffering. Of course, one of the most powerful ways to experience genuine happiness is to have an authentic encounter with another human being. Being heard, being accepted, being validated as a worthwhile human being, being treated with dignity and respect, being told that their life holds meaning and purpose. What enabled these unlikely relationships to form and thrive was the fact that their shared human longings were being met by each other. The superficial differences that usually separate one person from the next became irrelevant.

All the information I had accumulated that suggested supportive loving relationships were only possible between people who were similar to each other was shattered. It isn't our gender, families, interests, education, talents, strengths, socio-economic level, etc. that ultimately determine our ability to form fulfilling, lasting relationships. Our shared human longings are the threads that bind us to each other and that make it possible for people from every walk of life and corner of the world to look beyond differences to develop deeply fulfilling relationships with each other.

My theory about people being able to ignore their differences and connect through their shared human longings was powerfully confirmed for me when I experienced it firsthand in a most unlikely situation. I was at a business golf tournament, and following the round of golf, roughly 200 people gathered in the banquet hall for dinner. I was seated at a table with seven other people, six of whom I had never met before. As you might expect, the only thing we had in common was our shared participation in this business function. Typical of these events, people were talking about their professional roles and occasionally expanding on what their company was all about. I was completely disinterested in these conversations and was looking forward to eating so that I could get out of there at my earliest opportunity.

As I was eating, two fellows at my table were talking about their roles in their advertising company. I was trying to tune them out when one of them, sitting directly opposite me, suddenly looked straight ahead and said in a heart-felt voice, "I don't know what I'm doing in this job anymore." The way he said it immediately penetrated my consciousness, and I intuitively realized that this man was crying out to the universe for help. I focused all my attention on him and while looking him straight in the eyes said, "I completely understand how you feel." The look on his face was one of desperate gratitude. He began to vent his frustrations, describing the wasted effort, creativity, and passion he had poured into his job only to discover that at the end of the day he felt completely empty on the inside. Knowing that my value was to simply witness his story, I encouraged him to continue, and for the next 10 minutes he shared his frustrations, disillusionment, and sadness. He was coming to a turning point in his life and he knew that he couldn't postpone some serious decisions any longer, regardless of the costs. He felt he was close to giving up on life, so great was his sadness.

During his monologue, the fellow beside him would intermittently give him a jab and say something sarcastic or make a "joke" in an attempt to make him stop talking in such a serious way. Both the man who was sharing and I completely ignored his associate and focused entirely on each other while his story unfolded. For all intents and purposes there was no one else in the room. It was as though we had entered a sacred space where the usual rules of social intercourse and self-disclosure didn't apply. It was a space of complete safety, non-judgemental witnessing and complete respect from one human being to another. As he began to wind down his sharing, his associate suddenly turned to him and said: "You know, I've actually been thinking a lot of the same thoughts." Well, you could have knocked me over with a feather. It suddenly became clear to me that this annoying associate was feeling very uncomfortable with the direction of the storyteller's monologue. It had been triggering uncomfortable feelings within him. When his attempts to derail the conversation failed, he came to realize that this was a truly safe arena to share, without fear of ridicule or judgement. Once he felt safe, he decided to take the chance to honestly share his own doubts and fears.

I will never forget that encounter as long as I live. In the most improbable setting, with a group of total strangers, one human being reached out and connected with another human being and eventually were joined by a third who engaged in an honest dialogue of shared fear, frustration, and longing. The connection transcended every apparent difference and obstacle, and created a transformative moment of trust, safety, dignity, and respect between human beings. We were all changed through our shared encounter and authentic connection.

It was at that moment I knew, in the core of my being, everything that we imagine separates us from one another is an illusion. If we are able to simply set our superficial differences aside or, better yet, ignore them, what we discover is that we are all on a common journey of seeking and struggling. We're all longing to connect through our shared human yearnings. When we are able to see, acknowledge, and respond at the level of our common yearnings, we are able to make the powerful connections of authentic communication and communion. The fruit of that communion is an encounter of the most profound and life-affirming kind. The greatest gift one human being can give another is to see beyond everything we think makes us different and connect at the level of our shared human longings. This is what every human being has in common. Our yearnings for acceptance, unconditional love, and authentic connection are the foundation upon which deep connections and lasting friendships are built.

EXPANDING SELF-AWARENESS

1. Have I noticed how I tend to associate with people who are similar to me in some way?

2. What longings have I noticed all people share in common?

3. Have I ever found myself in a situation where superficial differences became irrelevant?

4. Am I becoming aware that our shared human longings are the threads that bind us together?

5. Can I recognize that addressing human longings is the foundation upon which authentic connection and lasting friendships can be built and sustained?

APPLYING SELF-AWARENESS

On a sheet of paper write: "If I was able to see beyond the things that I think make us different, I would..." Complete the sentence ten times, identifying how your perception of others might change. On the backside of the same sheet of paper write: "If I was able recognize that all human beings share the same human longings, I would..." Complete the sentence ten times identifying how this understanding might change the way you relate and connect with others. Answer the following questions.

1. What emotions come up for me from this exercise?

2. Based on what I learned, what—if anything—will I change?

3. What do I hope these changes will do to improve the quality of my life?

CHAPTER TWENTY-TWO:

WE HAVE NO IDEA HOW MANY PEOPLE
ARE IMPACTED BY OUR ACTIONS

Experiences like the connection I made at the golf tournament are the wonders that can occur when we choose to come from an unconditionally loving place. My ability to recognize and separate that man's reaching-out from all the noise and distraction of the event is one example of how our Higher Power enables us to help each other on our shared journey.

Everyone involved in that encounter experienced a powerful sense of connection, compassion, safety, and unconditional love. We were able to have the most intimate, life-affirming exchange in the most unlikely of environments because each of us, to the best of our ability, saw through the things that made us different and focused exclusively on our shared human longings. By creating a safe environment for those men to speak, I too gained the benefit of an unconditionally loving encounter. Every word I shared with them was equally applicable for me. This is how we can recognize when an authentic interaction is occurring—we gain as much benefit from the interaction as the other does.

When our deepest intention is unconditional love, our thoughts, words, and actions reflect that intention. This is how intimate connections occur. This is not to say that everything and everyone you approach will respond lovingly in return. We have no control over how others will respond, and it is none of our business. The very act of coming from an intention of unconditional love ensures that, regardless of how others choose to respond (and it is a choice they make whether they realize it or not), our experience will be positive.

I shake my head when people compliment me for authentically connecting with them, because the paradox of unconditional love is that to experience it you need to give it away. That is how Unconditional Love multiplies Itself. Unconditional Love can only multiply when conscious beings choose to invite It into an encounter. The truth is that when we help someone, we simultaneously help ourselves. Through making a conscious decision to extend unconditional love within an authentic connection, we too experience unconditional love.

The common denominator of all people who choose to come from a loving or unloving intention is that their deepest intention sets in motion conditions that will cause that intention to expand. Many of the outcomes from our exchanges occur when we are not around, but occasionally we get immediate evidence of the impact our deepest intentions create in the lives of the people we meet (like the experience I had at the golf tournament). Others we may not learn about for years, if ever.

I remember receiving a letter from a cousin I had lost contact with twenty years earlier. She wanted to express her gratitude for the power of my example, which she said had a powerful and beneficial impact on her life. I was flabbergasted. As we had had no contact for many years, it never occurred to me that anything I was doing would have the slightest impact in her life. From this event I realized that even people far removed by time and distance can still be impacted by our choices. I suspect that if you examine your own life, you too can recall similar revelations.

Everything we do counts! Everything we do ripples out into the universe. The questions we need to ask ourselves are:

- What kind of energy am I sending out into the universe?

- Is it loving or fearful in nature?

- Is it increasing the chance for others to awaken to the qualities and characteristics that affirm their life or the characteristics that trigger their fear?

I am not suggesting we are responsible for how others respond to us, but I am aware that we are absolutely and exclusively responsible for our output. Our intentions enter the world and have expanding consequences for us and for every life we touch. Our output either expands love or fear, and the energy of both arises from our intentions.

So, let's be clear. We are responsible for output not outcome. The outcome is none of our business because it's largely beyond our control. It is the business and journey of each person and their Higher Power to respond to the world they encounter. At times it may seem to us that people are making choices that are bringing them tremendous suffering. In these circumstances we need to be mindful not to simply jump in and try to "fix" them. As we'll see in the next chapter, sometimes our hellish experiences are the most effective teachers we have to show us how to experience a happier, healthier, and more fulfilling life.

EXPANDING SELF-AWARENESS

1. When I step into today, what is my deepest intention towards the world and myself?

2. What is the risk of determining my output based on a desired outcome?

3. What can I do to remember that I am responsible only for my output?

4. What can I do to remind myself that the outcome is out of my control?

5. Do I recognize that regardless of the outcome, my output enables me to honour what I value most in others and myself?

APPLYING SELF-AWARENESS

Make a list of intentions you believe would enable you to maximize your effectiveness as a human being consciously serving Unconditional Love. Following that, answer these questions.

1. How would my perceptions and behaviours change if I brought these intentions into my daily interactions with the world and myself?

2. What emotions come up for me from this exercise?

3. Based on what I learned, what—if anything—will I change?

4. What do I hope these changes will do to improve the quality of my life?

CHAPTER TWENTY-THREE:

SOMETIMES THE QUICKEST WAY TO HEAVEN IS BACKING OUT OF HELL

There are two ways to get 100 miles east of your location. One way is to head east. The other way is to head west. While one way is much shorter than the other, both will ultimately bring you to the same destination. In much the same way, if our goal is to develop the understanding, skills, and capacity necessary to experience a happier and more fulfilling quality of life, we can choose to learn from the wisdom and experience of others, or we can choose to head off on our own and explore all there is to explore, accumulating information and wisdom along the way. The first choice will advance us in the direction of our destination much faster and with less suffering while the second choice entails a significantly longer journey and considerably more hurdles to overcome before reaching our destination. Who's to say which direction is more effective or necessary for the development of our potential?

While it might seem obvious that following the wisdom and guidance of those who have taken the journey before us would be the more prudent and effective choice, I have met a great many people who, like myself, have chosen to set out on their own, who have endured significant suffering and, as counterintuitive as it might seem at first glance, declare that they wouldn't have traded all their difficulties for the easier, quicker path because of the lessons they learned along the way. They describe a journey of discovery that has taken them to the gates of hell, and with their backs against the wall they decided that this was not the place they wanted to be in their life. They about-faced and headed in the opposite direction. They further assert that they needed their hellish experiences to secure for themselves that the choices they were making were not bringing them the results they desired. It was only when they were backed up against the gates of hell that they finally began to make different choices to move their life in a different direction.

It seems that many of us require a degree of pain and suffering in our life to finally accept that the choices we are making are the very choices that are producing our pain. Despite what we've believed and acted on until now, the choices we've made have not brought us the quality of life we want, and we have finally come to accept that they never will. We finally realize that we need to release these ineffective assumptions, mental models, and unworkable strategies so that we can make more effective and life-affirming choices to move our lives in the direction of meeting our deepest desires.

I am not advocating heading west to get 100 miles east. I'm merely pointing out that either direction provides the life lessons we need to ultimately reach our destination. One set of choices moves us towards our destination by drawing on the collective wisdom and experience of those that have come before us. The other leads us to the hellish experiences we need in order to learn for ourselves what works and what doesn't. Often we discover what we want by identifying what we don't want. If you ask people, what they want you will often hear them say: "I don't want to be poor." "I don't want to be sick." "I don't want to end up alone." People who have experienced suffering in their lives seem to be keenly aware of what they want to avoid. It takes a certain shift in thinking to turn that perception around to define what we *do* want. The shift might sound something like this.

- Since I know that I don't want to be poor, then how much financial security *do I want,* and what am I prepared to do to earn it?

- If I don't want to be sick, what level of health *do I want,* and what am I prepared to do to achieve it?

- If I don't want to end up alone, what kind of relationships *am I seeking,* and what am I prepared to do to secure them?

Regardless of the choices we make, and the pain and suffering we create in our own lives and in the lives of those we encounter along the way, we are never so far from our destination that we can't make different choices.

This leads us to the central point of this chapter, which is that many human beings do their most substantial learning and growing as a result of their suffering. While most people don't set out to deliberately experience suffering, it would be a grave mistake to suppose that suffering is without value and to be avoided at all costs. Nothing could be further from the truth. As we've discussed, pain and suffering can stimulate our thinking in the most profound and life-affirming ways by showing us, in the starkest possible terms, the natural and logical consequences that result from that thinking. In our pain and suffering we are motivated to ask: "What the hell is going on and how can I stop this pain?" If we have the humility to own our suffering—to see that much of it arises from our assumptions, mental models, and behaviours—then we have broken through a powerful delusion that suggests it is people and things outside of us that are responsible for our pain. The more accurate truth is that our own perceptions, feelings, expectations, and actions have been the driving force behind much of our suffering and have led us to this moment of clarity and decision.

Even physical suffering that is not directly the result of our thinking and actions is significantly influenced by how we choose to interpret it. As we discussed earlier, there are things that happen in our life over which we have limited control, but even these instances give us the option to choose our responses. This is why it is so important not to relieve someone of their hellish experience. It is precisely our suffering that teaches us, in a most powerful way, what our perceptions, feelings, and actions have created and what we can do differently to get a more positive result.

It is never easy to see another human being suffer, but it would be a mistake to imagine that the only course of action is to relieve their suffering as quickly as possible, for to do so would be to relieve them of the discomfort they may need to break through their own ineffective assumptions and mental models to discover, for themselves, that the solutions they've been holding onto are not serving them well. At that moment of realization, Unconditional Love is waiting to provide them with a new thought, a new perception, a resourceful response—but only if they are willing to consider it. We can learn a lot about the most effective ways to support each other by taking our cue from the Universe, which is always available to us for the asking but will never violate our right to run our life by our own will... even if our will is taking us to the gates of hell.

EXPANDING SELF-AWARENESS

1. In what ways have my assumptions, mental models, and actions taken me to the gates of hell?

2. What did I discover about my choices and the experiences that accompanied them when I reached the gates of hell?

3. How have my struggles helped me finally accept the need for change?

4. In what ways has suffering been a positive tool for examining my choices and in helping me make more effective choices?

5. Do I recognize that as painful as it may be for me, the most loving freedom I can give another is the freedom to take themselves to the gates of hell so they can experience the full consequences of their choices and then decide what—if anything—they want to do differently to get a different experience?

APPLYING SELF-AWARENESS

Take a sheet of paper and draw a line down the middle of the page. On the left hand top of the page write: "Things I don't want." On the right hand top of the page write: "Things I want more of." List the things you don't want and want more of, then answer the following questions.

1. What is the positive opposite of the things I don't want?

2. How can I bring more of these positive opposites into my life?

3. Since what we focus on expands, how can I begin to shift my focus from the things I want to avoid to the things I want more of?

4. What emotions come up for me from this exercise?

5. Based on what I learned, what—if anything—will I change?

6. What do I hope these changes will do to improve the quality of my life?

CHAPTER TWENTY-FOUR:

LESS IS MORE

I would be failing you if I didn't point out that taking this journey will change the number of people you have in your life—people that you have considered friends up to now. Choosing to challenge the assumptions you have been operating under and deciding to live more authentically will be upsetting to some of the people you have associated with in the past. Some of these people may be quite close to you, and losing their friendship will be difficult as any loss is difficult. The reason some people may reject your journey and try to convince you that you are making a mistake is because of the threat your growth represents to them.

As my drinking progressed, I found myself changing friends. I grew increasingly uncomfortable with social drinkers who "didn't know how to drink" and began replacing them with people who drank like me. The reason I changed friends was obvious. My social drinking friends started making me feel more and more uncomfortable because they were perfectly happy having one or two drinks over the course of an evening whereas I wasn't able to stop drinking until all the booze was gone. Hanging out with social drinkers revealed the unmistakable difference in how much I was drinking versus them, and I didn't want to admit that my pattern of drinking was getting out of control. The only option I had was to change the people I hung out with. By shifting my "friendships" to people who drank the same way I did, I was able to deny that my drinking was getting out of hand. I was able to maintain the illusion that my drinking wasn't that bad, which allowed me to continue drinking alcoholically while preserving the fiction that I still had my drinking under control. This is how my alcoholism flourished while I fooled myself about the severity of my addiction.

As you begin to challenge the assumptions you have been living under, and start to live more authentically, those people who prefer to stay as they are will become increasingly uncomfortable around you in the same way as I became increasingly uncomfortable hanging out with social drinkers as my alcoholism progressed. At first they may try to convince you that you are being brainwashed by some new age rubbish or that you are being totally naïve—the world doesn't work that way. They may ask why you're turning your back on them. As you continue your journey, they may become so threatened that they try to stop your progress by accusing you of thinking you're better than the rest of the world, by saying that if you continue with this ridiculous journey, no one will to want to have anything to do with you.

While you are in the early and vulnerable stages of transition from a sleepwalking life to a fully conscious life, you may be filled with self-doubt. "Perhaps they are right. Am I making a terrible mistake?" Despite knowing that the way you've been living hasn't brought you the authentic happiness you've been seeking, at least you've had company along the way to share your disappointment. Now you are facing the prospect that even this small comfort is about to be taken away from you. Is it any wonder that you have doubts about continuing your journey?

As difficult and sometimes painful as these experiences are, they actually represent concrete evidence of the real-world progress you are making in your journey. In the same way that I became increasingly uncomfortable hanging out with social drinkers as my alcoholism progressed, the people who are trying to talk you out of your journey are becoming increasingly uncomfortable with you because your life is showing them how unconsciously they are living and your presence in their life is a constant reminder of the compromises they are making on a daily basis. Until they are willing to make similar changes in their lives, you are going to represent a threat to their status quo, and they will not want you as a constant reminder of how they are choosing, or refusing a conscious life. To reduce their fear and discomfort, they are going to do everything in their power to stop your progress. Failing that, they will desert you for people who are living the same way they are living so that they can preserve the illusion that everything in their life is fine—they don't need to make any changes.

Other people's rejection of you has nothing to do with you and every-thing to do with them. My social drinking friends didn't do anything to deserve my rejection. It was my discomfort being around them and my refusal to acknowledge that my drinking was getting out of control that moved me to replace my social drinking friends with alcoholic "friends" who didn't make me feel uncomfortable. Those who reject you are simi-larly motivated. It is not that you are doing anything wrong by choosing to live more authentically; it is that by doing so you are a constant reminder that *they* are refusing to grow. Your growth is a threat to them, and they must either stop your progress or find other people who are content to live the way they are currently choosing to live.

As difficult as this period of change may be for you, take heart. While your old friends may choose to stop being around you, others will begin to show up in your life. They will encourage and support your journey of growth, and you will find that while the number of friends declines, the quality of friendship you experience will significantly increase. Sleepwalking company will be replaced with genuine, vibrant friendships that you can count on when you need them. These friendships won't be based on hiding from the truth but on fully embracing and exploring the potential for personal and spiritual development.

There are more sleepwalkers in the world than there are people willing to live a fully awakened life, and while the quantity will always be against you, the richness of those relationships you discover along your journey will more than compensate for those who no longer feel comfortable in your presence. You are not becoming a snob and you are not rejecting those who don't want to be around you any longer. You are simply refus-ing to live a sleepwalking existence any longer. That is not a crime. It is a precious gift to yourself and to everyone who will be positively touched by your expanding unconditionally loving energy. Choosing to live from an unconditionally loving nature is the journey every individual in the world is invited to take and is the only means for reclaiming the life we lost along the way.

Don't be surprised if some of those who originally give you a hard time, or reject you because of the changes you are courageously making, meet you at some future point along your journey and wish to reconnect with you. If and when this happens, it is because they too have decided that a sleepwalking existence is no longer acceptable for them—they too have chosen to take their own journey of self-discovery and self-recovery.

As was stated earlier, you have no idea how your commitment to personal growth will impact others. Stay true to your growth, and the Universe will bring you the people you need to support you along the way. You will wonder why you were so afraid and waited so long before starting on this life-enhancing journey.

Be at peace and trust that the Universe is aware of your needs and will always support you when your deepest intention is to encounter and expand your own unconditionally loving nature outwards into the world. This is your deepest nature and your most compelling task. It is filled with challenges and fears, all of which will be overcome by continuing—one day at a time and to the best of your ability—to bring unconditional love into your life and the lives of everyone you touch. You will never be alone so long as you focus on embracing your own loving nature. This choice will attract others who are similarly motivated, and you will discover each other as kindred spirits, willing and able to assist each other on your shared journey of living a more authentic and genuinely happy life.

EXPANDING SELF-AWARENESS

1. Am I noticing that some of my old friends are visiting me less often?

2. Have people been trying to talk me out of my journey?

3. Can I see how the changes I am undergoing may be making old acquaintances uncomfortable?

4. Can I let old relationships go, knowing that the Universe will bring new relationships into my life that will be richer and more authentic?

5. Can I extend the gift of understanding to those who reject me and pray that they too eventually get sick and tired of living a sleepwalking life so that they will meet me again at some future point along my journey?

APPLYING SELF-AWARENESS

Take a sheet of paper and draw a line down the middle of the page. On the left hand top of the page write: "People who are supporting my change."

On the right hand top of the page write:"People who are not supporting my change." Answer the following questions.

1. Which people in my life are encouraging and applauding the changes I'm making?

2. Which people in my life are discouraging and criticizing the changes I'm making?

3. How are my changing perceptions, assumptions, mental models and behaviours impacting my interaction with others and myself?

4. Who can I share my findings, considerations, and emotions with to support the changes I am making on my journey to reclaim the life I lost along the way?

5. Which relationships do I want to strengthen and which do I want to release so that I can continue my journey towards greater alignment and authenticity?

6. What emotions are coming up for me from this exercise?

7. Based on what I learned, what—if anything—will I change?

8. What do I hope these changes will do to improve the quality of my life?

CHAPTER TWENTY-FIVE:

PARTING THOUGHTS

Thank you for taking this journey with me. More importantly, thank your-self. Together we have travelled the path to a greater level of awareness and understanding of who we really are beneath the story we have been telling ourselves all our lives. Throughout this book I have attempted to present and illustrate that you, and all other sentient beings, are far more than you imagined. As your awareness expands, you will discover and recover resources, gifts, abilities, and talents that you may not have realized you had or that you forgot in your quest to increase happiness and reduce suffering by seeking changes outside yourself.

Throughout this book I have referred to a better quality of life that awaits the discovery and recovery of your unconditionally loving self by putting your ego in the conscious service of your spiritual nature. So what do I mean by *a better quality of life*? Do I mean a life of ease and comfort? The end of struggle and hardship? An uninterrupted unfolding of joy, abundance, and bliss? No. Even if such a life were possible (and I've never met anyone who has such a life), I wouldn't wish it for you. A life of ease is a life of boredom. Once you've tasted every treat and purchased every toy, what then? Even the delight of the most delicious chocolate cake loses its appeal when you've eaten too many pieces. Nor would I wish for you the end of struggle and hardship, for without these all too familiar human con-ditions we would never discover our true capabilities, strength, resilience, and stamina. It is through struggle and hardship that the full scope of our potential is realized, as the purest of metals are refined in the fires of a blast furnace. Neither would I wish for you an uninterrupted experience of joy, abundance, and bliss. Were such a condition possible, it would mean the permanent loss of the emotional gift these qualities provide when they do appear in our lives. Without the darkness, we would have no appreciation of light; without struggle, we would have no frame of reference for the joy of triumph; without loneliness, we would lose our appreciation for authentic connection. It is only through knowing one that we can truly appreciate the other. It is the wonder of our human imperfection that excites our imagination to strive for a better quality of life.

The better quality of life I have been referring to is the understanding and realization that you are far more beautiful and capable than you have believed you are. It is the realization that the love and happiness you are seeking is within you, and the way you can access it is by noticing the qualities and characteristics of people, places, and events that awaken your joy, enthusiasm, and gratitude. Embrace and extend these qualities and characteristics in your daily life. The journey you are taking is a process of discovering and recovering your individual qualities, talents, and gifts. As we begin to notice and express these talents and gifts in our daily lives, we start to experience a sense of expansion and excitement, of wonder and possibility. It doesn't matter how "good" we are at expressing our talents and gifts by the standards of the outside world, all that matters is that we are encouraging ourselves to develop and express them in our own lives. Through us, they expand into the lives of those we touch. These qualities, talents, and gifts are expressions of Unconditional Love that each of us possesses in utterly unique forms. The more we honour and nurture them, the more alive and meaningful our lives begin to feel.

My deepest hope is that this book has awoken you to a view of yourself that is far more accurate, effective, and life-affirming than the life you imagined you possessed, the life you felt powerless to change when you began this journey. I pray that you have discovered the critical insight that you are not what you have done up to now, nor are you what has been done to you. You have not been living and experiencing the full measure of the life you were born to live. Through the lens of self-compassion, I hope you accept that everything you have done, thought, or felt made perfect sense based on the sum of everything you learned, believed, and experienced. You did the best you could—with the resources you had at your disposal—to increase your happiness and reduce your suffering. If you could have done better, you would have. What you may now be awakening to is the realization that you've always possessed the inner resources to experience joy, happiness, connection, meaning, purpose, and unconditional love, you just didn't know how to access them. Now that you are considering that you are not who you thought you were but are, in fact, a spiritual being arising from Unconditional Love having a human experience, everything you thought was beyond your reach is possible because the resources you need to bring them into your life is within you patiently waiting for you to invite them into your daily life.

The ideas expressed in this book are not the end of your journey; they are the beginning of it. Growth, development, and change are ongoing features of every human being who aspires to experience the fullest expression of wonder, challenge, joy, and fulfillment, which are the fruits of a consciously directed life in the service of Unconditional Love. The person who finished this book is not the same person who started it, because through the thoughts, emotions, and reflections you have experienced, you are no longer living in the dark nor are you willing to accept that your happiness—a better quality of life—depends on things outside of you changing.

Your journey towards the life you have secretly hoped you could live begins by accepting that you are absolutely and exclusively responsible for every experience you have, based on how you choose to interpret and respond to the conditions you encounter. No one or thing can bring you the love and happiness you seek without your conscious cooperation. Getting in touch with your own unconditionally loving nature and then doing everything in your power to extend it into your life and the lives of everyone you touch through your unique qualities, talents, and gifts will ensure that whatever the conditions you encounter along your journey, your experience will be a perfect reflection of the perceptions you are holding, the resources you are accessing, and the responses you are making. If you don't like the experience you are having, then the remedy lies within. You have the one power no one can take from you—the power to respond as you see fit. And if you don't like the results of one response, you are free to make a different response when a similar situation arises in the future.

You are a manifestation of Unconditional Love in physical form. You are interconnected with everything and everyone in the Universe, and with that which is not the universe but that thereby the universe exists. You have the option of consciously connecting and aligning your ego with Unconditional Love, and to the extent you choose to do so, the full resources of the Universe are suddenly made available to you for the sole purpose of enabling Unconditional Love to experience and express Itself through you. This is the purpose for which you came out of the Universe. To the precise degree you act in alignment with this purpose, you will experience the realization of your highest potential and the fulfillment of your deepest longings.

May you have the wisdom, compassion, and willingness to discover the beauty and wonder of your own true nature so that you and everyone you touch is enriched by the extraordinary gift of your unique and irreplaceable life.

May God, as you understand Him/Her/It, bless your journey of awakening from the slumber of misunderstanding, and grace you with the full realization of the unique expression of Unconditional Love that you truly are to yourself and the world beyond.

REFERENCES

Frankl, V. (1959, 1963). *Man's search for meaning.* New York, N.Y: Pocket Books.

Leslie, R. C. (1965). *Jesus and Logotherapy.* Nashville, NY: Abingdon press.

Losang, R., (2014). *The Four Immeasurables.* Reprinted from: Chenrezig Tibetan Buddhist Center of Philadelphia, Daily Prayers. Retrieved from http://www.tibetanbuddhist.org/prayer-refuge-and-bodhicitta-four-immeasurables

Kierkegaard, S. Retrieved from https://www.goodreads.com/author/quotes/6172.S_ren_Kierkegaard

King, M. L. Jr. Retrieved from http://www.goodreads.com/quotes/136038

Orsborn, C. (1995). *How Would Confucius Ask for a Raise?* Avon Books.

Phillips, D. T. (1998). *Martin Luther King Jr. On Leadership.* New York, NY: Warner Books.

Senge, P. M. (2006). *The fifth discipline: The art and practice of the learning organization.* New York, NY: Doubleday/Random House.

Wilber, K. (1998). *The marriage of sense and soul.* New York, NY: Random House.

JOHN PATERSON

It is uncommon to be with someone and to have the pleasure of experiencing parts of oneself mirrored back. Being with John Paterson creates a joy of experiencing yourself as loveable and loving. It is very special. John walks his talk of loving unconditionally. In fact, unconditional love is the essence of his spirituality. To find himself where he is today, John has taken a long and at times arduous journey. The middle child of seven siblings, he became an alcoholic at a very young age. Later, he found new maps that directed his travels into the corporate/consulting world, academic world, family world, and beyond. John earned a Master's degree in Leadership and is currently the Director of HR and Business Operations at LDR Holistic Addiction Wellness Centre in Langley, British Columbia. The journey, not the destination, is what John holds sacred. Eternally questing, reflecting upon his "Inner World" and his "Outer World," recognizing available choices, and finding the courage to act upon them, defines John's current journeying. This, and more, he does with the greatest of gusto! He is a passionate, energetic, exuberant man, and he brings all of himself to everything he does. His life-long passion is discovering how human beings can access and express their deepest and broadest potential. He is also a gifted musician, devoted family man, and a lover of nature. John is reflected in every page of this book.

Printed in Canada